THE

LONG

YES

WHAT OTHERS ARE SAYING ABOUT "THE LONG YES"

Faith-filled. Impactful. Empowering. Vulnerable. Powerful. Compelling. These are but a few adjectives to describe the missionary journey of Henry and Betsy in this book. This book is a must read not only to those who are called into full time missionary service but to both young and old in the faith. It is life-changing!

Ruby Bayasen, Asian Center for Missions, The Philippines.

Henry and Betsy embody authenticity, humility, faithfulness, and an unwavering commitment to Jesus and His cause. This book offers an inspiring account of their journey of obedience, sacrifice, and continual learning. It is engaging, deeply personal, and wonderfully readable. The stories will make you laugh, bring tears to your eyes, but above all, they will stir your heart to serve God with wholehearted devotion. Henry and Betsy's story is a powerful reminder that God delights to accomplish extraordinary things through seemingly ordinary people who trust Him and follow His lead.

Ps Bruce Hills, Former International Director, World Outreach.

The Long Yes is a warm, funny, and deeply faith-stirring window into frontier missions, showing how God delights to use very ordinary people in improbable places. These stories will make you laugh, move you, and quietly challenge you to say your own 'long yes' to Jesus, wherever He may lead. I heartily commend this book and pray that many believers who wonder whether God could ever use them will be drawn into His global purposes.

Dr Sam Ngugi, PhD. Director, Mission Campaign Network.

An invaluable sharing from a yielded heart that serves God in complete obedience. We highly recommend this book for those preparing for cross-cultural mission work as it gives great insights when stepping into new frontiers with God.

Kang Hoe & Margaret Yee, Former WO director, SE Asia.

Cross-cultural mission requires a special breed of person with a compelling call on their lives. Henry and Betsy are one such couple who have been willing to endure the challenges in service of others. This book will be a blessing and encouragement to all who read it and take to heart its message.

Charlotte Teal, Member Care services, World Outreach.

Henry and Betsy have been vital members of our community for many years. I've seen firsthand their steady faith, passion, and their "long yes" to God's leading. In this book, they draw back the curtain on their journey, sharing with honesty and humility what it has meant to walk with Jesus over a lifetime. Their stories are rich with hard-won wisdom, humor, and practical lessons that speak to everyday life and the Great Commission. As I read this book, I laughed, cried, and gave thanks to God. I'm confident the insights they offer will encourage you and enrich your own journey as well.

Ben Brooks, International Director, World Outreach.

This book is a treasure for both new and experienced missionaries as well as senders back home! It is a real and honest account of God's faithfulness and a family's commitment to obey His calling. From the richness of their mission experience and their walk with God, their training courses were birthed and developed by these seasoned missionaries who have said Yes and are still saying Yes to God's calling.

Marina Prins, Member care consultant.

This book describes the trials and triumphs of missionary life, and it reminds us that reaching the lost involves lots of prayer and hard work.

Dr Don Fisher, Didasko Missions Academy.

Get ready for a wild, inspiring, and faith-filled journey through the intimate stories of a couple who clung to a faithful God while living among the unreached.

Ps Andrew Sieberhagen,
Global Missions Pastor, Heritage Christian Church, USA.

"Lord, here I am—send me!" …and then what? If that cry has ever burned in your heart, you NEED this book! From the first page you'll be captivated by jaw-dropping true stories of radical trust, answered prayer, and miracles through the most ordinary people—stories that will set your faith on fire and leave you longing for more of Jesus. Don't wait—grab it today and watch God turn your ordinary life into an extraordinary God-story!

Dr Wynand (Wayne) de Wet,
Founder and Director, One Plus God Ministries.

Get this book! It is a tremendously good read – by turns intriguing, funny and deeply challenging. Henry and Betsy are the real deal. They have proven God's faithfulness through thick and thin over decades of giving Him their "Long Yes". They are a wonderful team, even in the way they co-write this book, drawing out great truths through honest storytelling, amusing anecdotes and poignant sharing, all of which draw you in to follow their journey and learn from their insights. (We highly recommend their online training platform 'Didasko Missions Academy' as well.)

Ross and Christine Paterson,
Antioch Missions/FieldPartner International.

THE LONG YES

Missionary Stories of Potholes, Chickens and a Faithful God

Henry Vermont
Betsy Vermont

The Long Yes: Missionary Stories of Potholes, Chickens and a Faithful God

© 2025 Henry and Betsy Vermont

Editor: Charmain Kleu

Front Cover: Esté Hupp, https://www.estehupp.com/

For permission or corrections, email   henry.vermont@dasko.org

Unless otherwise noted, Scripture quotations are from the Berean Standard Bible (BSB). Officially dedicated to the public domain as of April 30, 2023. Produced in cooperation with Bible Hub, Discovery Bible, OpenBible.com, and the Berean Bible Translation Committee. Access on the web: https://bereanbible.com

ISBN 979-8-218-84467-7

Dedication

To our awesome and faithful God, Jesus our Hero, *for from Him, and through Him, and to Him are all things. To Him be the glory forever* (Romans 11:36).

To our two beloved children, Esté and Adriaan, who carried their crosses with us into the unknown, and followed Jesus with courage and trust.

To our faithful partners in prayer, financial support, and encouragement, who also said "Yes" and journeyed with us from the very beginning.

To all the unsung missionary heroes we know by name, who quietly and sacrificially serve among the unreached in hard places—your faithfulness speaks louder than words, and your lives continue to inspire us.

A note on names of people and places

For security reasons, some names of people and places have been changed. Publishing the real names of former Muslims and missionaries still serving could put them in danger. To protect all involved, the authors write under pen names.

TABLE OF CONTENTS

CHAPTER ONE

THE BEGINNING

———— ⟨∞⟩ ————

The two men from the island

Henry, Mozambique

When I opened our front door, my heart skipped a beat. Even though it was still early in the morning, the air was thick with the unrelenting tropical heat. In the distance, I could faintly hear the sound of fishermen calling out to their helpers and the rhythmic thumping of women pounding rice.

Before me stood two large strangers. They wore full Islamic garb—spotless white robes reaching their ankles, Muslim prayer beads in their hands and *gofia*[1] caps set firmly on their heads. They looked very solemn. I could tell this was about something serious and important.

"This is trouble," I thought, knowing that only the strict imams[2] dressed like that, and never when they came to visit me.

At that moment, a jumble of thoughts popped into my head: What am I even doing here? How did I ever manage to get myself into this situation?

To answer those questions, we have to go back—back to the very beginning…

---

1   Cap worn by Muslim men
2   Islamic leaders

Saved by grace

Henry, South Africa

About ten years before, we were living in suburban bliss, living the dream—our own man-made dream. I was in my early thirties and had my own successful software company. I was determined to become rich and retire early. I had it all: a beautiful wife and two smart kids, and a huge house with a swimming pool and three cars. Our business's small office block was adjacent to the front of the house so I didn't even have to commute to work, like the others in the rat race have to. We had pretty much everything we needed. I was in charge —the king of my castle. Life was good.

Even though I'd grown up in a traditional Afrikaans-speaking church, I was a closet agnostic. In fact, I despised religious people, especially pastors. My secret opinion was that they were parasites of society, preying on people who were gullible.

Betsy

I came from the same church background where being a Christian mostly meant being a "cultural Christian." It was something you did on Sundays, almost like belonging to a club. But deep down I was convinced there had to be more to faith than what I had come to know: dry sermons, mostly from the Old Testament, and tedious, dull singing. I sensed something was missing in my life. I knew it had to do with God, though I just couldn't quite put my finger on what it was.

Henry

We had a fantastic marriage, except on Sundays. Betsy wanted to go to church, hoping to find that missing link, and I just wanted to sleep in, hoping to avoid contact with "Christian hypocrites." Because I loved her so much, I ended up going to church with her most Sundays. That was, until the day I decided I had had enough.

That morning, while getting ready for church, I just couldn't stand the idea of having to sit in a church, adorned with suit and tie in the African heat, listening to someone talk about stuff I really didn't care about. "This is the last time we go to church," I told Betsy. "If nothing happens today, that's it. I can think of a million better things to do on a Sunday."

Then Betsy told me that she had seen a sign for an English-speaking church nearby and suggested we try going there. She said, "Maybe if we hear it in English, it will be different." Not that we knew what that "it" was. Our mother tongue was Afrikaans, our kids were in an Afrikaans school, and our friends were Afrikaans-speaking. We even had an Afrikaans Bible somewhere in the house. Up to that point I had never opened it. And now we were going to an English-speaking church? We just hoped the family would never find out as this would certainly be frowned upon.

All our preconceived ideas about church would soon be shattered on that Sunday morning. First of all, they did not meet in a church building, they met in a school hall. The word "sect" immediately came to mind. Not a good start. But, to my astonishment, I noticed that the people were dressed informally. No one was wearing suits and churchy clothes like we were expected to wear at our previous church. As quickly as you could say "tie," I had mine off!

Right at the start I was very skeptical of everything there. Everyone was very friendly. Why? What did they want from me? Surprisingly, I could tell that they actually really wanted to be there! That was just plain weird. We stepped into the school hall, totally out of our comfort zone. I was sure everyone could see that we had no clue of what was going on or what to do. There was a lot of talking and laughing before the service started. That was strange, too.

An older lady sat at a piano. Where were the pipe organs? Then a white-haired pastor walked to the front to complete the picture. We had definitely walked into a trap. And then everybody started singing, accompanied by the lady playing the piano. I stood there in amazement as they sang, because I could see that these people really believed what they were singing about! I thought, "They might be naive for actually believing all this stuff, but at least they are sincere." I could live with that. Only years later did I realize they were worshiping in spirit and in truth. But that day my eyes were still blinded.

Betsy

By the third line of the very first song, tears were streaming down my face. I didn't understand what was happening, but deep inside I knew that I had finally found what I'd been searching for. The rest of the service passed in a daze. I was overwhelmed, confused, undone. Then the white-haired pastor closed his sermon with a simple explanation of the gospel. And there it was—the missing piece. Jesus! It was Jesus!

I had walked into that school hall hopeless, frustrated, and lost. I walked out a new creation. It was as if my life, once flat and gray like an old black-and-white movie on TV, suddenly burst into brilliant color.

"One thing I have asked of the LORD; this is what I desire: to dwell in the house of the LORD all the days

of my life, to gaze on the beauty of the LORD and seek Him in His temple." (Psalm 27:4)

Henry

I went home that day with many questions. I experienced and saw things that totally pulled the rug from under my feet. Many things that happened in that service challenged my preconceived notions. Betsy had been transformed, and I could see the difference. She was no longer depressed. She glowed with an inner joy that was radiating out of her, like a light that was switched on. She had never had that before. As for me, I at least was totally fine with going to that church with her—no ties and suits, and friendly and sincere people. Sunday after Sunday the white-haired pastor taught us many things that started to make me think. But most of all I went along because I wanted Betsy to stay that happy.

Colin, the pastor, and his wife Marina gently persuaded us to attend the Alpha Course that they presented. Little did I know that this course is aimed specifically at skeptics like me! I peppered poor Colin with cynical questions and dumped all my years of church frustration onto him. To his credit, he stood his ground. Eventually we became lifelong friends with him and Marina, so much so that they ended up being our spiritual parents.

I was shocked when I learned that he had been a bank manager but had given up his good job, position and a huge salary to become a humble pastor of a small church that met in a school hall. That did not fit into my cynical worldview of pastors as "parasites." In the meantime, the Alpha Course was giving me a lot to think about, and my unkind and barbed remarks and questions gradually became more honest. They started to take on a sense of urgency.

During this time, we took a short holiday at the seaside. One day, while I was body surfing, a wave dumped me onto the beach, and I cracked a vertebra in my neck. After that incident I was in constant pain. I went to doctors, chiropractors, took medicine, even wore a neck brace. But to no avail. I was still in constant pain. I didn't sleep well, I couldn't concentrate on my work, and I was miserable. My business started to suffer. I needed to concentrate to do my work and develop software, but the pain was relentlessly distracting me.

Then I remembered that there was a man at one of the companies I consulted for who had the reputation of praying for sick people who then got healed. I used to scoff at that possibility and avoided him like the plague because he was one of those "fanatic Christians." But now I had become curious about faith *and* I was desperate. Finally I decided I had had enough of this agony and one day, after work hours, I plucked up the courage to go and ask him to pray for my neck.

He eagerly agreed. I braced myself for what was coming. I didn't know what such "crazies" might come up with. Maybe they would shout, jump up and down, wild eyes, and even foam about the mouth! But I decided I would endure whatever happened on the off chance it just might work. I was that desperate. Gently, he put his hand on my neck and prayed a short prayer asking God to heal my neck in Jesus' name. As he prayed, I felt heat coming out of his hand on to my neck. And suddenly all the pain was gone! I was so relieved that the pain was gone, but I left for home in a confused state. My logical brain couldn't explain what had just happened.

That night I slept like a baby for the first time in three months because I had no pain. When I came into the office the following day, my secretary remarked that I looked much better. "I had a good night's sleep," I explained, dismissing the prayer of the previous day. In fact, I was waiting for the pain to come back because apparently it all must have been merely psychosomatic. The man had given me attention and kindness that had made me feel good, and so the pain went away. I was feeling better because of the good sleep, I told myself.

However, three days later, I was sitting in my office when I realized that the pain had not come back. I worked out that he had prayed for me for maybe thirty seconds. Could it be that "coincidentally," after three months of suffering, the pain had disappeared during a prayer lasting only thirty seconds? The probability of that happening exactly just then was statistically insignificant. Basically impossible.

At that moment, I knew it was God who had healed me. I just couldn't deny it anymore! There was a God. And He cared enough for me to heal me, even in my unbelief, cynicism and with me being so judgmental.

From that moment on I was His, and He was mine. Forever.

Whom have I in heaven but You? And on earth I desire no one besides You. (Psalm 73:25)

Visions of more

Henry, South Africa

Shortly after we gave our lives to Christ, we were hit with a staggering truth: Millions of people in this world have never heard the name of Jesus and may never know His love. That knowledge burned in our hearts. The only problem? We weren't preachers. We were just normal people. I was a computer geek, and Betsy was a librarian. If you needed any software program or help with finding books on dolphins, we were your team. Preaching? Sharing the gospel to the ends of the earth? Not so much.

But we had one nagging question: What could we do to help?

We tried different ways of sharing the gospel in our neighborhood but saw little fruit—unless you count awkward conversations or people excitedly telling us that they were already Christians. We didn't know there were so many Christians in our neighborhood. We thought everybody was as lost as we had been.

Then came an opportunity that changed everything. We attended a training course on how to use the Jesus Film as an evangelistic tool in informal settlements. Was this God's sense of humor sending a computer nerd and a librarian to show movies to people in the bush? But it was during that training that He showed us that He could use us. And moreover, that He even *wanted* to use us.

This is where we first learned that besides coincidence, there's something we call a "*God-incidence.*" That is when something is so coincidental that it had to have been orchestrated by God. You will be reading of many *God-incidences* in this book.

Through one of these *God-incidences* we met an older couple, Coen and Denise, who were seasoned veterans in the Jesus Film ministry. They became our mentors, patiently discipling us for lifelong ministry. More about them later.

You are there—<u>you</u> do something

Betsy, South Africa

I was waiting in the car for Henry and the kids near a taxi rank. The sun had almost set. The air was thick with smoke from fires people had made in rusted old rubbish barrels. They were warming themselves around the fires, talking, looking like silhouettes. A few minibus taxis were parked haphazardly, waiting for customers. I was casually looking at this scene of life playing out before me. The strange thing about silhouettes is that you can see what is going on, but you can't see the detail. Everything becomes almost surreal, like a scene from a movie.

I noticed a man, only because he started walking. Well, I shouldn't call it "walking." Let's just say he was moving, pushing a plastic crate in front of him. He was using it as an aid to stay upright but moved very awkwardly. He had to walk bent over, because the crate was not much higher than his knees. "Drunk," I thought.

The sun had set by now and it was getting dark. The only light came from the smoldering fires and faraway streetlamps. The man moved again, very slowly. I don't know what made me pay more attention, but I started to watch him with more interest.

As he came closer, I could see him clearly. And then it dawned on me. He was not drunk, he was hurt! The way he was holding onto the crate, while pushing his leg forward was a clear indication that he had a physical problem. That man was injured, and he was using the crate as a crutch.

My casual interest changed into concern, and then into compassion. I felt so embarrassed for judging him earlier. I started pleading with God, "Lord, please heal that man," and

"Lord, look at him, it is so heartbreaking," and then "Do something, Lord!"

Then I heard the Lord gently whispering: "*You are there, you do something.*"

What? I was dumbstruck! Had I heard what I thought I'd heard? The logic behind it was so real, I couldn't deny it. The excuses came quickly: It's dangerous out there. It's too dark. I am not strong enough.

"Lord, please do something!"

The irony hit me like a ton of bricks. I love to pray "Lord, use me," "Jesus, I am Your servant," "Lord, make me more like You." And now, when He does give me the opportunity to serve Him, to be His hands... then I fervently pray and ask *Him* to do something! Loving obedience to Jesus' commands actually means that I should get my hands dirty too, not just my knees.

A wise man once said that God left poor and suffering people among us so that we can practice being merciful.

Oh, I need to practice a lot more!

"For I was hungry and you gave me something to eat, I was thirsty and you gave me something to drink, I was a stranger and you took me in, I was naked and you clothed me, I was sick and you looked after me, I was in prison and you visited me" (Matthew 25:35-36).

Nature miracles and the Jesus Film

Betsy, Africa

We started showing the Jesus Film in remote areas of South Africa, Zambia and southern Mozambique. The Jesus Film strategy was brilliant: The film is shown on an open piece of ground, often an informal soccer field. We had a projector with four huge reels of film, a generator and two tall poles that we would set up with guy lines. A screen was pulled taut between the two poles. On top of these poles were loudspeakers. People could sit on both sides of the screen to watch the movie. We usually drew sizable crowds. During reel changes, someone would preach the gospel, and after the showing, we did an altar call. Many responded.

Standard prayer for this ministry was to pray for the weather before the showing of the film, besides praying for people to be saved and set free. If it was very cold, or it rained, or there were strong winds, it could jeopardize the showing. Too cold or rainy weather would keep the people away. Strong winds could tear the screen or it could simply topple over.

Seeing how God answered our prayers about the weather at many of these showings was almost too spectacular to believe. We always worked in teams, so everybody witnessed these miracles—it was not just our imagination. The Jesus who calmed the storm was still the same.

Jesus Christ is the same yesterday and today and forever (Hebrews 13:8).

Once, just as we arrived at the place where we planned to show the movie, it started pouring with rain. We quickly carried all the equipment into the small church hall to start partially assembling it in a place where it was dry. At that time, a couple joined us on a showing. It was their first-ever evangelistic outreach. We asked them and the local pastor to begin praying while we set everything up. It was madness to consider showing the movie, because the rain was coming down in buckets. But we had such confidence that God would show up again that we never wavered. And sure enough, by the time we were ready to move everything outside, the rain had stopped.

Dramatic dark-blue clouds were building up. That meant even more rain. The team kept praying, while we set up the equipment. We kept on preparing the equipment, and when we looked up, there was a U-shaped clearing in the clouds directly above us, with the open side of the U far off in the distance. We could see the stars above us! And all around us was this thick, solid bank of dark clouds, with lightning flashes crashing down. It was the most dramatic event we had ever seen.

That night, the movie finished without any interruptions, and many people gave their lives to Jesus. Once we had packed up the equipment in the car and started driving off, a gentle rain began to fall again. Soon after that night, the man who had come along, started studying theology and became a pastor a few years later.

The heavens declare the glory of God; the skies proclaim the work of His hands (Psalm 19:1).

The praying mechanic

Henry, Africa

While we were doing short-term mission trips with the Jesus Film in southern Africa, we drove an old Land Rover. That Land Rover was my nemesis. I'm sure that thing was evil because it too often kept me under its hood, trying to fix things, rather than allowing me to be out there, evangelizing the lost.

It gave a smooth ride, but it leaked on the driver's foot when it rained. Dust came in everywhere. By the end of a day's driving on rough roads, we found sand in our ears, in our teeth, in our eyes... And this particular Land Rover had the habit of breaking down. Often. And mostly in the worst places, like in the middle of nowhere in rural Africa, right where there were no spare parts or good mechanics nearby.

Once we were on our way back to South Africa from an outreach, tired, dirty, but so grateful for what God had done during the trip, when—nothing. A dead Land Rover. All became quiet around us, only the wind rustling through some dried-out bushes next to the road. We were, predictably, in the middle of nowhere, with a very dead car.

Outwardly calm and collected, I climbed out, put on my overalls—which I always took along because it was as necessary as gas, oil, and water—and opened the hood of the car. "Start praying," I said to Betsy. In my mechanical ignorance I looked at the engine, hoping to spot something, anything, that I could fix. Pipes, wires, dirt and mud. More pipes. I wriggled some wires, checked that the cap on the radiator was tight, and sighed a lot.

But it was just me standing out there, in the heat and the dust, trying to deal with this situation. Betsy was still sitting in the car. I felt a bit neglected, because here I was, all on my own, trying to sort out this mess. I thought, she could at least lend me some moral support by standing with me, staring at the engine. We could stare at the engine together. I had no idea what to do.

Suddenly Betsy got out of the car, gave the engine one look and asked, "What's under that thing?" She pointed to a small rubber cover. How should I know what was under there?

I was getting annoyed with her. I'm trying to fix the car here! But dutifully I lifted the rubber cap—and there it was, clear as day. A loose wire! "How did you know that wire was loose?," I asked her, completely stunned. "I didn't," she said. "I saw it while I was praying in the car."

I rejoined the wire and lo and behold, the car purred like a happy lion when I turned the key. What a woman! What a God!

The Land Rover and the angel

Henry, Africa

At another time we were on a trip to show the Jesus Film in Zambia at some of the villages. Our infamous Land Rover had a roof rack. Those who have used one would know that one tends to overload it. In this case, we had extra gasoline in Jerry Cans that we tied on the roof rack. Very stupid, in hindsight! When those old Land Rover Defenders get top-heavy, they start to sway, especially when going through potholes.

We were on our way back to South Africa at night. The dirt road was extremely bumpy and full of potholes, but we could travel between forty and sixty km/h (twenty five to thirty eight mph). Suddenly, the car swung at an acute angle to the road, and we were thrown to the side of our seats. It felt like our car had swerved at a forty-five degrees angle. At that moment I was *convinced* we were going to roll. There was no other physical possibility.

Betsy just shouted: "Jesus!" The next moment, it literally felt as if a hand grabbed that car, picked it up and put it straight back down. We were back on the road again and the car was driving forward on the road. Our hearts were beating fast for an hour afterward! The impossible had just happened.

Looking back through the years, I realized I don't know how many accidents we have been spared from, if the Lord had not been with us. Betsy once jokingly said that she could just visualize angels hanging onto the car, hair blown back by the wind and wings flapping furiously, guiding the car all the time! Perhaps God let them work in shifts to give them a breather.

We can't help wondering what we're going to hear in heaven about situations where we didn't even realize we were in danger. I'm so looking forward to that. Come, Lord Jesus!

Not by works

Henry, South Africa

One time, I found myself in hospital in South Africa. My body was swollen everywhere—hands, feet and face. I had an allergic reaction to something. In the emergency ward, nurses were eyeing me like hawks for the onset of anaphylaxis.

We had just come back from an outreach to southern Mozambique, showing the Jesus Film. Obviously, I was allergic to something. Maybe the food we ate? Then Betsy figured it out: I had had an allergic reaction to the malaria prophylaxis I was taking.

It turned out the doctor in charge was a Christian. That was good news. I expected to have great discussions about the lost and the Great Commission. Then he said something to me that really shook me.

"You know, you don't have to do these things to be saved," he said. "We are saved by grace, not through works.

Jesus did it all for us." I was stunned. Of *course* I knew that—and that was *exactly* our motivation for going to places where Jesus was not known yet. Those people also needed His grace!

We weren't doing this to *be* saved, but out of loving obedience to Jesus' Great Commission[3], and a passion to share His message of salvation with lost people.

> *How then can they call on the One in whom they have not believed? And how can they believe in the One of whom they have not heard? And how can they hear without someone to preach? And how can they preach unless they are sent?* (Romans 10:14–15).

Faith and a raisin finger

Betsy, South Africa

We were showing the Jesus Film in a remote area of South Africa, when a freak accident caused my finger to be crushed in the door of our Land Rover. The whole tip of my finger was a mushy mess. After hours of driving, we found a clinic, and *God-incidentally*, a seasoned doctor on duty. Jesus was with us, as always. The doctor gave the finger one look. Her diagnosis was that she could save the fingertip, but she would have to remove the pieces of nail that were still there, as well as the nail bed. She told us that no nail would ever grow again if she removed the nail bed. We didn't really have a choice. A finger without a nail it would be. Henry saw the nail bed coming out. Gross! But I was fine with that.

---

3 "Therefore go and make disciples of all nations, baptizing them in the name of the Father, and of the Son, and of the Holy Spirit, and teaching them to obey all that I have commanded you." (Matthew 28:19-20)

Months later, my finger had healed. It now looked a bit like a raisin—nail-less but functional. Our daughter Esté, twelve at the time, looked at it and declared, "Mom, us girls should have nice nails. I'm going to ask Jesus to give you a new one." Sweet kid. I actually didn't mind the missing nail so much—it felt like it was my war wound for Jesus—but Esté's faith was touching.

And wouldn't you know it, a few weeks later, what looked like an "infection" turned out to be a brand-new nail sprouting. The doctor had said it was impossible, but apparently Jesus disagreed… with a wink in Esté's direction.

Jesus is faithful. *Always.*

CHAPTER TWO

THE LONG YES

———— ⬤⬤⬤ ————

The calling

Henry, South Africa

While we were doing all these Jesus Film outreaches part-time, we completed the *Perspectives on the World Christian Movement* course. It was there that we learned about Unreached People Groups (UPGs). This immediately caught our attention because we were shocked to learn that there were entire ethnic groups in the world with little Christian witness. Either there were no Christians at all in these groups, or there weren't enough Christians to evangelize the rest of the group without outside assistance.

Later, when we lived in Mozambique, we saw the reality of the lives of an Unreached People Group firsthand. One afternoon, we stopped by a roadside stall where a man was selling odds and ends. Betsy asked him in Portuguese, "Do you know the Lord Jesus?" He paused, thought carefully, and then asked, "Does he live nearby?" That moment never left us.

The sobering facts are that out of more than 16,700 distinct people groups on earth, 41% remain unreached. That's 1.8 billion men, women, and children who will live their entire lives and then die without ever hearing the Good News that God loves them and that Jesus died for their sins. And this was now, today, almost 2,000 years after Jesus commanded us to go and make disciples of all *nations* (Matthew 28:19–20). *"Nations"* in Greek is the word *"ethnē"* from where we get the term "ethnic groups" or "people groups." That there were still so many of these groups yet to be reached shocked us[4]. We wanted to do something to help complete Jesus' Great Commission. This set us on the path to becoming missionaries.

By this time, we were seasoned in doing outreach with the Jesus Film all around southern Africa, over weekends and during our vacations. Life was good. We were serving the Lord. But what I wasn't telling Betsy was that something was brewing in my heart. The thought that people might live their whole lives and then die, never having heard of Jesus and salvation through Him, was fast becoming an all-consuming fire in my heart. This must be the greatest social injustice ever!

I was drawn to Isaiah 6. I read it over and over again, meditated on it, and prayed about full-time ministry. One day I could no longer hold it in. Overcoming my cowardice, I blurted it out, like Isaiah, saying, *"Here am I, Lord. Send me!"* (Isaiah 6:8). I was shocked at my own words. Breathless. I expected something like, "It's okay, I've got my people already." But I felt God's answer in my spirit: "Okay."

---

4   Unreached People Groups, https://joshuaproject.net/

For a split second, I wanted to swallow my words, bury them somewhere, pretend it never happened. Really? "Okay?" "No, no! God, what are you doing? I'm not a preacher. I'm not qualified." Yet I knew what I had heard. What now? This would become a life-changing moment in my life. For weeks I thought about my conversation with God. God had taken me up on my offer! Now what?

Eventually, I gathered enough courage. Hesitantly, I told Betsy that I had told God I was prepared to go into full-time missions, and He had said, "Okay." She calmly looked at me with a little smile, and said simply, "Good. I've known that for six months already."

We once asked a woman who was on her way to Taiwan as a missionary how she had known that she had been called to go to Taiwan. It was just so radical. Taiwan is on the other side of the world!

Calmly she replied, "I know it in my 'knower'."

We immediately knew what she meant—it was an inner conviction, an inner peace, the unshakable confidence of God's call and promises. Your spirit knows. Of course there had been many seeds sown in her life: prayer, advice from missionaries, research, and Bible studies. All had contributed to, and helped build up to this point. And now she was absolutely convinced of God's calling on her to go to Taiwan. And so she went.

And now we were in the same position. The topic of our conversations and our prayers totally changed. It was all about the future, missions, our children's future and Unreached People Groups. In our hearts, we knew that this was the right thing for us—we just knew it in our "knowers!" God soon confirmed our calling with this scripture:

You did not choose Me, but I chose you. And I appointed you to go and bear fruit—fruit that will remain—so that whatever you ask the Father in My name, He will give you (John 15:16).

Counting the cost

Betsy, South Africa

We were in the midst of narrowing down our scope of where to go. I told God I'd go anywhere—except for Mozambique. I was adamant, because about a year or so before, we had gone to southern Mozambique on vacation. There we had seen corrupt police, poverty, and the devastation left by the recent civil war. The primitive and harsh conditions were just too challenging for me. As for Henry, he'd go anywhere, just not to Muslims. He confided in me that he was simply a coward, intimidated by Muslims.

God must have been chuckling to Himself because that's exactly where He sent us—to Muslims in Mozambique! But He didn't force us to go there. He gently changed our hearts over time. In fact, He changed our hearts forever.

Through research and the leading of the Holy Spirit we learned about the Iso[5] people in Mozambique. There wasn't much information available about them, apart from the fact that they were Muslims, lived along the coast, that they were mostly illiterate, and that there were few believers, if any.

The northern part of Mozambique was an isolated, war-ravaged area with land mines littered across the land and little infrastructure. At the time, the only way of getting there was by road—really bad roads. The country's trade language was

5   Iso is a pseudonym for the people group to protect believers from persecution.

Portuguese, so we realized that we would have to learn that to be able to get around in the country. However, the Iso people spoke Isoni[6], an undocumented tonal language. We would have to learn that, too. Learning two languages at the age of forty was a daunting task—a challenge—but we knew with God's help we could do it.

By then, our children, Esté and Adriaan were thirteen and nine years old respectively. How would they adapt? We would have to home-school them, as there weren't any appropriate schools in that area. The list of challenges was growing longer and longer—and so were our prayers, in both quantity and intensity. Would us "city slickers" be able to survive in that isolated, rural area as a family? Could we really do this? How could we even count the cost if we didn't know what the "cost" would involve?

We did not get much encouragement from family and Christian friends. The standard advice from Christians was to wait for more confirmation. An old friend even said we were having a serious mid-life crisis.

Henry's parents did not take the news well. Initially, his dad thought that our business was going under and that this new direction was Henry's way out. He even offered him money to help out with the finances. But when Henry showed him the business's financial statements, indicating that our business of sixteen years was booming, his father was angry at him for leaving all of that behind!

His parents were concerned about a lot of things. Our safety was a big issue for them, understandably so. As I mentioned earlier, Mozambique had just come out of a civil war and the country was in a mess. Apart from a lack of

6   Isoni is a pseudonym for the language of the Iso people.

proper medical facilities, the roads were damaged, bridges had been blown up, and the country was still riddled with land mines. We knew we would also have to face other logistical challenges, like unreliable communication and food of questionable nutritional value.

They were also concerned about their grandchildren's future, especially regarding their schooling. Henry's mother had been a teacher and the idea of home-schooling was anathema to her. She told us the kids would have no future growing up in Mozambique.

From their point of view, we were making a big mistake —and they told us that. So did others in our extended family. Despite these push-backs, we *knew* that God had called us to the Iso people. We knew it in our "knowers." Yet, we also wanted to be responsible. Going on an exploratory trip to the Iso to see for ourselves what the conditions were, and to confirm our calling, seemed the right thing to do. And so, we went.

"Which of you, wishing to build a tower, does not first sit down and count the cost to see if he has the resources to complete it? Otherwise, if he lays the foundation and is unable to finish the work, everyone who sees it will ridicule him, saying, 'This man could not finish what he started to build" (Luke 14:28–29).

Baptism of fire

Henry, Mozambique

The soldiers came rushing out of the bushes in camouflaged uniforms, aggressively waving AK-47's, yelling, shouting. I just froze. I had only a few words of Portuguese, but I understood what they were shouting "Spy! Spy!" I got arrested and marched off to a little drab building in the bush. They questioned me in Portuguese, in broken English, and with angry body language. I just stood there. This was way over my faith level. How had I ever managed to get myself into this situation?

It all started a few months before when we made the decision to go on an exploratory trip to Isoland[7]. There was a nearby town close to some of the Iso villages, and that's where we would base ourselves for the duration of our trip.

We planned on a three-month period, just long enough to help us get a feel for the area, see what food was available, what the living costs were and the like. I realized that we would have to stay in tents for those three months, too. But we were serious. If this is what God had called us for, we wanted to prepare and learn as much as we could before moving there.

The road to Isoland was, to say the least, adventurous. In those days there were no GPS devices or Google Maps. We only had a conventional map with minimal information. We also soon found out that the "National Highway," called the EN1 on the map, was often a dirt road, full of potholes, snaking through little villages. The warning signs for landmines next to the roads made up for the lack of road signs. We were warned that there was one stretch of 600 miles that had no gas stations. We needed to take some extra gas along. We had camping gear, extra gas for the car, and Jesus. With a lot of people praying for us, we started out on our journey.

It took us nine days to reach that town. (Later we broke our own record—four and a half days of driving for twelve to

7   In this book we call the area where the Iso people live 'Isoland'

fourteen hours. Efficiency, missionary-style). Midway there the car broke down. Again. Thankfully, we were close to a mission station. While camping there, we "accidentally" met a woman on the Bible translation team for the Iso language, who just happened to live in that town we were driving to. A *God-incidence*, I always say!

When we finally reached our destination, we realized that we had lost her address. Great. We were meant to meet up with her and she was going to point us to an obscure camping site in the area. All we could do was drive slowly through the town, population 140,000, asking around in broken Portuguese if someone knew her. It was like looking for a needle in a haystack. And then, a miracle again, our daughter spotted her walking down the road. She never walked there, she told us, but that day her car had broken down. *God-incidences* everywhere.

We found the campsite on the edge of town—bare bones, rustic, but safe. For the next few months that was home. We went exploring, which meant adventures like crossing a rickety bridge with clanking loose steel plates that had the kids screaming in fear. They swore they'd never go over it again. I had to break it to them: For us to get home, we'd have to.

During one of these small trip, we were on our way back to our base. We had one more night to go before getting back to the camp site. The owner of a little guesthouse in a small town which had an area for camping next to it, got inspired with a get-rich-quick scheme when he saw us. We could camp there, but at an astronomical price. We, however, decided we were not going to be part of his retirement plan. So, just outside of the town we put up our two little tents next to the road and slept there. The next morning, we woke up to a crowd of villagers surrounding our tents, pointing at us and excitedly repeating one word: "Simba!" Thanks to the movie The Lion King, we knew what that word meant. Lions! Apparently, lions were roaming around in that area. I was sure that, by now, God's angels protecting us must have been exhausted! But we got safely back to the campsite.

A few weeks later we were returning from another trip inland, showing the Jesus Film at the request of a local pastor. We had limited success. Besides a few others, there was one Muslim man that showed interest in following Jesus. But the following morning, when the pastor went to his house, the other Muslims in that area had already gotten to him, intimidated him and he no longer wanted to talk to the pastor.

We were finally on our way back to the town that by now was starting to feel a bit familiar. We would stay there a few weeks longer before attempting the last stretch back to South Africa. There were no roads on the map for that area. We had to guess where we had to go. And yes, we got lost. But while trying to find the right "road"—more of a track really—we saw an old, broken, rusted army tank in the field. It must have been a relic from the civil war of a few years earlier.

This was a great distraction. I'm an enthusiastic tank fan, so this tank became the backdrop for an impromptu family photo shoot. As the kids posed next to the tank, the unthinkable happened. A group of army soldiers stormed me out of nowhere and promptly arrested me as a spy. Apparently, that rusted old tank was sitting inside a military camp. Who could have known? To my credit there were no signs, no fences, nothing at all to indicate anything of the sort.

Nobody knew where we were. We had no communication with the outside world. How would people know what was happening? But God knew. While I was being interrogated, Betsy was sitting outside in the car with the kids, not knowing what was happening, and whether she would ever see me again. And then the Holy Spirit told her: "Praise God in all circumstances." With more boldness than she really felt, she told the kids, "We have to sing songs of praise. Now!" While sobbing, the kids tried to sing along with her. Just a few minutes later, I was released. Without any explanation, but minus my camera, which they confiscated as evidence of me being a spy. God again!

As we drove off, all of us were still shaking, the kids sniffing, but we were so overwhelmed with gratefulness. God was our refuge and strength, a very present help in trouble (Psalm 46:1). We drove away as quickly as we could. A short while later we found a little village that had a market. We needed food. Being a spy on a mission makes you hungry. The market was a chaotic scene with people, onions, bread, bananas. The four of us were walking slowly around the market when Esté yelled, "Thief!" I instinctively closed my hand over my pocket, barring a greedy hand who was reaching for my wallet. Despite this hiccup, we got some bread and were back on the road.

Just outside the village, yes again, the police stopped us at a "check point" (read "bribe station"). Everything got checked—tires, lights, papers, the level of tinting on the windows—as slowly as they could. We just hoped they didn't pick up that I was actually a spy. Our patience with this checking process was misleading. We simply had no energy left from the previous adventures. After some time, and with no bribes paid, we were finally on our way again.

We were still in the middle of nowhere, the only car on a dusty, never-ending road. The sun was sitting low, and I hoped that we would reach the campsite before dark when an ear-splitting rattling sound erupted from beneath our feet. We were soon engulfed in a cloud of dust. A dreaded feeling came over me. I slowly pulled the car over to the side of the road, switched off the engine, and just sat there for a moment, trying to think.

By the time I had my overalls on, and my tools out, there were already six or seven Mozambicans under the car. Where did they come from so quickly? Sure enough, the front shaft had broken off and hit the underbody of the car. With the help of these eager bush mechanics, we managed to saw off the shaft with a thin blade, because that was the only way we could get to the bolts. I gave them all the cash I had on me, and we were off again, but now stuck in two-wheel drive. We crawled into town just as the sun slipped below the horizon.

The next morning we wandered into the local market full of handmade furniture and housewares. While trying to gather prices to draw up a budget, a group of men started crowding around me. With the previous day's attempted robbery still fresh in my mind, I clung onto my wallet like it was a bar of gold. But they outwitted me—it was just a distraction. Their partners-in-crime were breaking into our car that was parked outside the market. They broke the front-door lock and took everything they could find inside the car. For the rest of the trip, I had to enter the car like a gymnast—through the passenger side and crawling over onto the driving seat.

Back at our tents, but now in the backyard of the Bible translator's house we met earlier on the road, I saw oil leaking from the car. Really? Is there anything else that could go wrong? Luckily, I came prepared with a set of tools to fix anything, plus putty, tape and glue. I was ready for any event. The oil was leaking out of a cracked sump pump. This Land Rover used automatic gearbox oil and my first thought was, where would I find more oil in a town where everybody drove manual cars? But I tried not to think of that obstacle and drained out the rest of the oil so I could use it again. My plan was to fix the crack with steel putty. But first, I needed to rest and get some coffee.

When I got back to the car, everything had been stolen. Everything—except the car. All my tools, the precious putty. Everything. This was not funny. I felt like Paul who wrote that they were under a burden far beyond their ability to endure (2 Corinthians 1:8). But again, through another *God-incidence*, there were people in town who lent me their tools. Someone else had putty and another person knew where I could get automatic gearbox oil.

After three months of exploring, adventures, misadventures, and a deeper level of praying, we were on our way back to South Africa, in two-wheel drive and with a sump pump containing a huge lump of putty. And then, the cherry on the cake, as they say. On a long stretch of road we got pulled over and were hijacked by a drunken policeman, waving a real AK-47 for real effect. He got into our car and forced us to take him to his home in a village down the road. When he got out, I just pressed that gas pedal right down to the floor and the car flew off, leaving a huge cloud of dust behind it, just in case he decided to shoot off a few rounds.

A few weeks after returning to South Africa, Liezel, our friend and prayer coordinator, shared a remarkable story. While we were away, another intercessor had urgently contacted her, insisting that everyone needed to pray for us *that* day. The call went out, and many did. Later, as we compared notes, we realized that it was that very same day I was arrested, and when the car broke down in the middle of nowhere. If they hadn't been praying, what would have happened? How great is our God!

Many people ask us why we went back there. The answer may seem oversimplified: It was our calling, loving obedience to a faithful God, and a passion to see lost people coming into the Kingdom. And perhaps a dash of "hero syndrome," which the Lord sorted out before too long.

This trip was far more than an exploratory visit. It was a baptism of fire. We realized from the first "mishap" that we were in for a battle. The devil was trying his utmost to discourage us from ever returning to the Iso.

He did not succeed.

Tower of trust

Betsy, South Africa

After we returned from our epic exploratory trip, we were even more set than ever on going to the Iso. And yet, while preparing to move to Mozambique, I started getting pre-field jitters. Counting the cost became very real.

We handed our sixteen-year-old business over to a colleague, while Henry took on consulting work during our final months of preparation. He needed to be flexible with his time to be able to raise up financial partners for us. Quite suddenly we didn't have a steady income anymore. This new way of looking at money was exhilarating, faith-building, but also very challenging!

We took our children out of "normal" school and I started home-schooling them. The idea was that we should be used to home-schooling by the time we arrived in Mozambique. Then schooling would be one less challenge to overcome. This was a good idea. Obviously it was God's idea! Later on we became quite good at doing school in a reed hut, or outside under a tree, or sometimes even by candlelight.

I still remember the day we went to the kids' school to inform the headmaster what our plans were. I was waiting in the school's office, looking at all the photos of the sports teams, and the other framed awards proudly displayed on the walls. My stomach turned and doubtful thoughts began to race through my mind. "What do we think we're doing? Taking our children out of 'real' school? Are we crazy?" The shocked look on the headmaster's face when we told him didn't ease my growing anxiety either. He asked me if I was a qualified teacher. I was not. But I put up a brave face and told him that God would help me. He responded with a skeptical expression on his face.

We also had to cancel our medical insurance. That company, as with all the others we approached, would not insure us while living in Mozambique. And rightly so. Proper medical facilities were not available there. From the insurance companies' point of view, we were a liability. That area was rife with malaria, cholera and other unpronounceable diseases. The closest qualified doctor was many hours' drive away during the first few years.

The insurance challenge was also true for our vehicle. The insurance companies we approached would only insure cars going into Mozambique on short trips. We realized that once we imported our car into Mozambique, we would have no insurance.

There were many other challenges to overcome too. One of the worst was having to help our children say goodbye to their friends and helping them to work through their fears and questions. I was struggling with my own issues, but to see the kids going through their's was very difficult. I was wrestling with God one day, telling him that our daughter was very talented in arts and drama. I reminded Him that she would not be able to receive any further training once we left. In hindsight, I was not trusting God for the impossible.

I asked God, "Don't you want what's best for her?"

"This *is* the best for her," God gently answered. I had to believe Him, and I wanted to, but it was so difficult. I felt guilty, too.

I thought to myself, "We are not even on the mission field yet! What will we have to face once we get there?" All these issues we had to face, and criticism from well-meaning people started to have an effect on my thoughts and mindset.

The defining moment came when we sold our house. The house was in my name, so I had to sign it over to the new owners. As I was signing the documents, it felt as if my heart dropped into my stomach. I could feel it sitting there! I thought to myself, "There goes our last security." I felt very vulnerable and almost fearful. Yes, yes, I know. Where was my faith in God, and my reliance on Him? I felt a bit like Peter, jumping out of the boat, and then moments later sinking in fear. In that moment of crisis, in the presence of an excited new homeowner, a satisfied estate agent, and my children running around oblivious of my inner turmoil, God flashed a picture into my head.

I saw a tower of blocks, the kind small children play with. The blocks were piled up high and I saw myself and Henry sitting on top of this tower of blocks. The tower was unsteady and was swaying a bit. It looked like it could topple over any minute. Then I saw God's hand come into the picture, plucking out a block lower down the tower. The block had "finances" written on it. The blocks dropped, but the tower remained standing. The tower became shorter. Then God's hand came again, plucking out a block with "insurance" written on it. More blocks dropped and the tower became even shorter, but sturdier. The next block out was the "schooling" block. God's hand continued to pluck out blocks from underneath us. As the tower became shorter and shorter, it also progressively became steadier.

At last, I heard God saying to me very lovingly, "I am taking away everything you are relying on. I want you to rely only on Me."

Immediately, I became calm. In the midst of emotional turmoil, only God's peace can do that. God showed me that our security was in Him alone. I could focus again on the future, with an unspeakable joy and peace in my innermost.

I am not against medical or other insurances. In fact, years later in Southeast Asia, we took out medical insurance again, because we could. But at that time God showed me the unsteady tower of worldly trust I had built. He wanted me to understand that ultimately our security should be built only on One Block—God our Rock.

Number seven

Henry, South Africa

We were almost there, ready to leave for our new lives with the Iso. Apart from selling the house, I had given away my business, home-schooling was going well and we had sold our cars, except for the truck we would use in Mozambique. We had joined a missions agency, World Outreach[8], and started raising financial support. Everything was falling into place.

By the way, joining a reputable missions agency is crucial for a missionary's longevity on the mission field. They will provide you with missionary training, help you prepare to go to the field and give you strategic guidance and pastoral care once you are there. Most of all, they help you to remain accountable on the field. World Outreach is such an agency. We owe them much after these many years.

Yet, even after all our preparations, I had this nagging feeling that God had made a mistake in sending me.

One day, having just come home, I remained sitting in the car, arguing with God about this. I felt that I just had to explain to Him exactly what He was getting into by sending me. I explained that I was a computer geek—a city boy. I suggested to Him that He rather send more of a macho-type person, a rugged adventurer, someone who likes the rough outdoors and camping, and knows how to fix a car.

Years before, when friends would invite us to go camping with them, I would decline the invitation quickly, saying, "My idea of roughing it is slow room service!" So here I was in the car, reminding God that I was a city boy and a computer geek, not a macho man.

---

8   World Outreach, https://world-outreach.com/

As I was going on like this, God suddenly dropped these words into my spirit: "You were not my first choice. The others had all said no." I was stunned, shocked. And I somehow knew I was the seventh person He had asked. The others all said no.

Immediately I realized that if I was number seven, and so unqualified, what would number eight and nine and the rest look like if I said no? But I knew that God would not love me less if I said no, too.

In that moment of shock, I humbly said again, "Here am I, Lord, send me." From that moment on I was more determined than ever. I knew by faith that God had a plan for me, and that He had chosen to use me.

This was *The Long Yes*.

The test

Henry, South Africa

Now I'm not one who gets many visions. Especially not one that plays out like a movie. That is why this vision took me by surprise.

Preparations were underway for our move, and I was still steadfast in my resolve that I would follow Jesus wherever He led. As I was praying one day, I saw myself being driven into a dead-end alley by a group of angry Muslims. There was no sound in the vision. I saw how I backed up against a wall. There was nowhere to go. In their hands, these men all carried stones. I crouched down against the wall and held my hands over my head as they started stoning me. I saw this play out, but I didn't experience any pain.

Suddenly, I heard the Lord's voice. "Are you sure you really want to do this?" Not for a second did I think that this was prophetic in any way. I knew the Lord was helping me to face the potential consequences of what we were doing. As I saw myself there against the wall, I felt an incredible and unexplainable calm overcome me. Faith rose up in me, and I said to the Lord, "Yes." I know that I could not have said this out of my own strength and courage. It was He who gave it to me in that moment. God would give me all the inner power I needed to face whatever circumstances were waiting for me.

Thankfully, this event never transpired.

Teamwork

Betsy, South Africa

As part of our preparation, we gathered a team of volunteers in South Africa—our core support team—led by Charles as the coordinator. They faithfully took on vital tasks for us: rallying prayer support, securing home-schooling materials, arranging accommodation during our visits, managing our finances, and distributing our newsletters. Their behind-the-scenes service is woven into our story. You'll see their contributions throughout this book.

And just like that, our move to Mozambique was underway!

CHAPTER THREE

FROM TENTS TO TABLES

An adventure or a nightmare?

Henry, Mozambique

We were finally on our way. A few friends offered to make the trip up to Isoland with us, taking some much-needed supplies for us that would help us start our new life with the Iso. We learned a lot from our exploratory trip and felt a bit more confident about the trip. But now we had to think not just about ourselves, but also about the four cars and trailers following us.

During the Mozambican civil war, many bridges had been blown up. We had to cross a river close to such a blown-up bridge, which was in the process of being rebuilt. Even though it was the dry season and the river was but a trickle, it was raining. The surface of the road had turned into a muddy, slippery mess. The road led to the bottom of the riverbed, where someone had put planks on top of the rocks so the construction workers could cross the river. Because there was very little traffic in those days, the construction workers let us go over too.

The only snag was that the banks of the river were quite high. And steep. Really steep. We had no choice but to drive down a steep incline of about five stories on a narrow road that descended sharply, with a number of hairpin bends along the way. This was a muddy dirt road with the driver's side facing an almost vertical drop of many meters down to the rocky riverbed. Considering that we were pulling a heavily laden trailer, the descent to the riverbed and ascent up onto the other side was quite a hair-raising prospect.

Betsy happened to be driving at the time when we came upon this river. We couldn't stop and change drivers because we might have gotten stuck in the mud if we did. The best thing to do was to keep moving. Betsy was "it." In a panicky voice she said, "What should I do?" I told her that the car was already in four-wheel drive and that she should just go for it.

So she did. Down the slippery inclined road and its hairpin bends we went, then over the bumpy planks on the riverbed rocks. As we neared the end of the planks, the riverbank on the other side loomed large before us. The road looked the same: narrow, steep, muddy, with hairpin bends. We could see the muddy rainwater running over the side of the inclined road on the riverbank facing us.

Again she said with a near-hysterical voice, "What must I do now?" "Hit the gas!," I said with also a somewhat unsteady voice. I realized that if we were going up that steep road, and we lost momentum and traction along the way, the whole car and trailer combination would start slipping back down, and the trailer would jackknife on that narrow road. We would then also slip down the incline to the edge of the narrow road. Obviously, there were no barriers on the side of the dirt road, so we would roll over and drop several stories down. At that moment I hadn't expected my imagination to run that wild. Just remembering and writing these words is increasing my heartbeat and making my breath shallow.

Betsy hit the gas and up we went. Up, around a hairpin bend, up the next stretch, then the next bend, and around the next bend, up again... Afterward, our friend in the car behind us, told us that he had been watching with bated breath how the trailer went around those bends on one wheel.

All the while, we were praying that the Lord would stop the rain so that the roads would be dry for the rest of the trip. In the meantime, the driver behind us was praying that it would rain more, because he was having so much fun slipping and sliding in the mud. For him it was the adventure of a lifetime. You guessed it. He was one of those macho guys! One can't help wondering whose prayer the Lord was going to answer and whose not!

Incidents like this made me coin the phrase: *"There is a very thin line between an adventure and a nightmare!"*

When we got to the top, Betsy kept on charging ahead, so much so that we lost sight of the other cars behind us. We didn't want to stop in case we got stuck. As soon as we got to a place where it was safe, we stopped in the middle of the dirty muddy road, shaking and giggling nervously. We couldn't pull off to the side of the road because the construction people had scraped the dirt road recently, creating a two- or three-foot-high dirt mound all along the two sides of the road.

Eventually, the car behind us came into view. I noticed all his wheels were locked, yet the car was steadily sliding toward us, managing to stop just behind our car. The driver was smiling broadly and was obviously having a huge amount of fun. Then he asked me, "Did you see the land mine sticking out of the side of the mound next to the road? The rain must have washed the top layer of soil from it." No, I had not seen it, thankfully. Scary. What a reality check. Thank you, Lord, for your protection!

Once the rest of the convoy had arrived, I took over from Betsy as our driver. The road was so slippery that the car was slithering along, like a crab, at about a forty-five degrees angle to the road, with the trailer jackknifed in the other direction. Of course, we weren't going all that fast. There was no time to look at the speedometer, so I have no idea of what our speed was. But we were cruising along quite happily (yet nervously) like that. Until suddenly, the wheels got traction on a patch of drier ground.

We abruptly shot over the top of that mound on the side of the road, trailer and all, crashing down the other side of the mound and into the bush with me hanging onto the steering wheel for dear life. And there we went, dodging trees and bushes and rocks. Ironically, there was better traction off the road than on the dirty muddy road. Yet I knew I had to get back onto the road, because we had just learned that this area had uncleared land mines! But I also realized that the mound was so high that if I drove across it slowly, we could end up being suspended on top of the mound, with the mound between the front and back wheels. There was only one macho thing to do. I told Betsy and the kids to hold on tight as I was going to go over the mound at an angle, but at speed. I put my foot down on the accelerator and we flew across that mound, crashing into the mud on the road, slithering back and forth.

Can you imagine the exhaustion that overcomes you after more than ten hours of such driving? Then you need to be up at four o'clock the next day for another day of driving. Thankfully, not all the days of driving were that extreme, but no day was easy either.

I was so proud of our kids on this trip. They were absolutely amazing. So well behaved and patient, it was almost unbelievable. In fact, on this same trip, they got into a minor argument at one of our stops one day. Ernst, one of the men in the convoy, saw the argument and went up to them, shaking each one's hand in turn saying, "Congratulations! I'm so grateful to see that you are normal kids. I was just thinking it's impossible that kids could get along as well as you had."

My God is stronger

Henry, Africa

The border post between Mozambique and Malawi—how could one describe it? Two words almost do it: utter chaos.

Crossing land borders with a car was never simple. Passports, customs, import papers, random fees and all demanded at once, in a place that looked like a bomb had just gone off inside a tatty, small office. No queues. No signs. Just a sea of people pushing, bargaining, shouting, all desperate to get through as fast as possible. All pressed together like sardines in a can. I remember once feeling that the man behind me wasn't wearing underwear.

And in that chaos, theft thrived. Leave anything unattended, and it vanished. But what could we do? I felt uneasy to leave Betsy and Esté alone with the car. Yet we couldn't all go to the little office and leave the car and trailer unguarded either. We had a year's worth of food and school supplies in there, as well as cash and medicine.

That's when the hero of the day stepped up, our ten-year-old son Adriaan. He insisted on guarding the car. Through the dirty windows of that dingy office I kept my eye on him. There he stood, our small little man, planted like a rock beside our vehicle and trailer, shoulders squared, hands planted on his hips, glaring at the crowd as if he could take on an army.

The faith and courage of that young boy! He stood firm, just like David before Goliath.

Camp life

Henry, Mozambique

Camping in Mozambique was not quite like camping in a developed country. We had some interesting and amusing experiences there. Twice we had to camp for extended periods: once during our exploratory trip to Isoland, when we camped for three months in tents, and then again for a couple of months when we moved there.

The toilet facilities were not exactly the most hygienic. A "long drop" in Africa is an outdoors, no-frills version of basic indoor plumbing. It has a deep hole in the ground with a cement lid on top and a hole cut in the middle of this lid. The hole looks like a large keyhole. Add a bamboo fence around it for privacy, and voila—your very own throne.

Except that there is no flush handle, no porcelain seat. In fact, there is no seat at all. And definitely no reading light. Creature comfort considerations are simply not part of the design. You don't sit, you squat. And you don't flush, you just... trust gravity. It's simple, efficient, and a hundred percent eco-friendly. Oh, and if the hole is big enough, *echo-friendly* too.

The "showers" in the camp were, let's say, cute. There were two large drums of water in each cubicle, one was on a stove that heated the water on a small coal fire, and the other one with cold water. With a small bucket, you scooped up some hot and some cold water to get the water to an ideal temperature and then you poured it over yourself.

One evening, just after Betsy got into bed, the chief of security (a dog) decided to stake his claim to the tent by lifting his leg against it, at the spot right next to Betsy's head. The camp puppy also felt safe with us and proved it by regularly vomiting up his food next to our tents. A monkey did the same from out of a tree, right onto Betsy's windbreaker! She seemed to be a favorite target for this kind of activity. A crow sitting in the same tree relieved himself on her shoulder one day. Splat. Good shot!

At night, we could hear the dogs drinking the dishwater left over from washing our pots and pans outside the tent. A monkey took the bread out of a plastic bag and had a feast one night. The same monkey had an irritating habit of shrieking loudly directly above our tent at two in the morning. It was an intelligent monkey because from the night we put some stones on the table for throwing at him, he never shrieked again.

There were bugs. A lot of them. On one day Betsy caught six sand fleas feasting on her in under five minutes. The kids and I had an animated discussion on why the fleas seemed to prefer Betsy. Maybe because she bathed more than Adriaan. Well, most people in the world bathed more than Adriaan. However, his attitude toward the concept of bathing improved dramatically one day. Someone in the campsite told us about all kinds of worms one can contract while camping if you didn't wash regularly, or did not wear shoes. In a flash, we saw Adriaan making off toward the showers, sandals on his feet and soap in hand.

After two months of drastic... I mean rustic camping, the missionary we had met on our exploratory trip, invited us to set up camp in her backyard. That was a great upgrade! No more drunken choruses keeping us awake at night. No more sharing showers with questionable backpackers. And, best of all, some actual privacy.

But the toilet? Still a long drop. And this one came with an additional feature. Bees. Yes, a full colony buzzing happily down below as you nervously go about your business. Our efforts to relocate the bees were less than successful. Eventually, we did what missionaries are supposed to do: we prayed, while spraying bug spray down the hole, closing the lid as quickly as we could.

Extraordinary kids

Betsy, Mozambique

At the local campsite, our kids received some unexpected education that was not part of their home-school curriculum. It was a crash course in human behavior, namely how alcohol reduces one's ability to sing in tune or hold intelligent conversation. Well, not the abilities of the kids, but of the people who came to drink at the campsite bar.

On weekends, the owner of the campsite and bar would start a generator which switched on all the lights. For us, sleep was not possible. So, we had tea in the dark, watching the "show" in the illuminated bar and restaurant area. We made the best of our grandstand seats (our fold-up camping chairs) and decided to use it as an educational opportunity for the kids. Adriaan, ten years old at the time, even wrote an essay for home-school about what happens to someone when they drink too much alcohol. He wrote, "… they start talking louder, they go red in the face, take off their shirt, get on the table to dance. Then they fall down."

Spot on! I gave him a top grade for his report. This was an aspect of home-schooling we had never anticipated. But it worked. Our kids were never interested in alcohol after watching others disgrace themselves because of it.

The kids also developed an impressive prayer life, mostly by praying *for* rain. For when it rained, the bamboo school hut we used at the camp site was a sieve, which meant —hallelujah—no school that day! Later on, when we lived in an Iso village, they knew that rain still meant no school, because their schoolroom was on a veranda enclosed with only burglar bars and mosquito netting. So when it rained, we couldn't use the school room. Well, we could have used the dining room, but hey, what an opportunity for an off day.

They were good minefield spotters too. The whole of Mozambique was dotted with land mines, a leftover from the civil war. At some places along the road, you could see sticks planted in the ground, with white and red paint at their ends. These sticks were put there when someone had "discovered"—the hard way—that there were still land mines in the area. The kids were able to see these sticks long before we could. In our area there were two minefield clearing companies who were constantly removing land mines.

The kids became experts in doing school by candlelight. We often did not have electricity, and when it was a cloudy day, it was dark in the house. So, out came the candles. Once,

45

a generous supporter gave us a whole box of candles from South Africa—only, the South African candles were not used to the heat in Mozambique. Even without being lit, they bent over, looking like sad little ladies with arthritis. But school we did.

For years after that, I suffered from an aversion to candles, especially if they were meant to be romantic. Once you've had to use candles for everyday living, they lose their romantic appeal.

It broke our hearts to see how Esté missed her friends. She cried for three months straight in the beginning. But God gave her a "can-do" attitude. Over time, she adapted, made many new friends, learned Portuguese, worked hard at her schoolwork, and eventually finished school a year earlier than the average. She aced her SAT tests. We were so very proud of her.

Adriaan had some bad experiences. Once he was robbed by youths with a speargun who wanted the bag of cookies he was taking to a friend. Another time he was hit on the head by a stone from a catapult. He came home, blood streaming down his face. To witness this is not good for a parent's heart. After all, it was not the kids who had volunteered for this life. We had long conversations with the Lord about this.

Despite these experiences, both kids independently and long afterward told us that they could see that the experiences of living there had made them more mature and more resilient than the friends they had left behind in South Africa. We could also see it. Both did very well with their post-school studies, too.

They had learned to be strong and resilient, having faith in God and trusting Him in all circumstances.

Be rude to me...

Henry, Mozambique

We knew before we went that we would have to learn two languages: Portuguese, which was the trade language of the country, and afterward Isoni, the heart language of the Iso. Many Iso didn't go to school, so they didn't learn Portuguese. Most of them were illiterate. For them to really understand who Jesus was, they had to hear it in Isoni.

By this time, our tent days were behind us. We were living in a Portuguese-style house in a town near the Iso village where we planned to move once we began learning Isoni. But first, we had to learn Portuguese. After all, how else were we going to import our car, pay for water and electricity (when we occasionally had them), or charm our way through encounters with the traffic police?

At first, Portuguese felt daunting. A Latin-based language with gendered nouns and verbs that morphed into shapes our own language, Afrikaans, had never dreamed of. But there was hope. We had access to lots of resources for learning Portuguese, like dictionaries, books, programs and movies we could watch.

I was starting to get the hang of it—speaking nasally, confidently shifting word endings from masculine to feminine and even attempting those terrifying verb conjugations. I was feeling good. Hey, I was a true linguist.

One day, after coming back from a trip to South Africa, I was unloading the car. Because of the terrible roads, we always carried two spare tires—one bolted underneath the car and the other chained to the roof rack. When arriving back in Mozambique, I would always take the tire that was tied to the roof off, not wanting it to perish under the merciless sun. And tires were just too tempting for thieves.

But that roof tire was my nemesis. Being short, I had to balance precariously on top of one wheel, reaching up to unscrew the nut. It was a two-hand job, but the moment I let go with one hand, I risked falling backwards onto the ground. Clearly, I needed someone to steady me with a hand on my back.

So, spotting a man idling nearby, I confidently put my Portuguese into action. I called out and asked him to come "support me from behind." He froze, eyes wide, looking slightly shocked and bewildered. After a few moments of hesitation, he slowly came closer, gingerly placing a hand on my back, and the second the tire came free, he bolted like a startled rabbit.

Puzzled by his strange reaction, I grabbed my dictionary. And there it was: the horrifying truth of what I'd said. The sentence I'd so confidently used to ask for support actually meant, "Come and be rude to me from behind."

I'm so glad Jesus speaks Afrikaans...

The missionary, the rooster, and the water pistol

Henry, Mozambique

Any similarity between this story and any persons or chickens, living or dead, is purely coincidental.

Once upon a time, there was a missionary who, after a few months of camping, finally moved into a rented house in a town. He got to upgrade his sleeping arrangements to lying down on a real bed and not a camping mattress on the ground in a tent. The missionary loved his beauty sleep. All went well until the day his neighbors got a mega-sized rooster.

The rooster did not need any beauty sleep. He loved to wake up at between 2:15 and 3 a.m. in the morning. He would stretch his legs, flaps his wings a bit and proceed to crow his heart out to celebrate the new day. Loudly. Very loudly. It seemed that the rooster never understood that the new day was only due to break a good three to four hours later. God had created this rooster with the most amazing lungs. His crowing achievements echoed throughout the entire town, much to the delight of other roosters, who would happily join in. Try as they might, the others simply could not keep up with this rooster, as it really had a special gift: volume.

The missionary did not have much appreciation for the rooster's gift. Especially since the rooster's favorite perch was about five yards from his bedroom window. Empirical data gathered over the course of at least a week proved to the missionary that the rooster's crows came at an average interval of fifteen seconds.

This left the missionary with much time to think and give deep consideration to the events at hand. He thought long and hard about many deep theological issues, such as why animal sacrifice is no longer practiced. Can the sin of irritability be excused by lack of sleep? May one pray for the sudden death of a chicken or not? May one help facilitate such a death? How sinful is the harboring of murderous thoughts against chickens? Does Satan use dumb animals to attack and discourage missionaries? Worldly considerations also arose. Just how hungry were the neighbors? Did they have any food in their cupboards? How could these Muslims be convinced that this rooster would make the ideal meal without the missionary sacrificing his Christian witness to them?

Missionaries, just like other people, tend to sinfully take things into their own hands instead of leaving it to the Lord. In this case, it was the missionary's son's high-pressure water gun that the missionary took into his own hands. The rooster was very surprised when rain abruptly fell on him during the dry season, and he was stunned into silence by this unusual occurrence. But not for long. Soon the rooster fought back by attempting to reach a new level of volume. Pavarotti would have been put to shame.

Then the happy day arrived. One morning, another majestic crow turned into a squawk. This was followed by a short, sharp crack. No more crowing. Ever again. The missionary hoped that the neighbors had enjoyed an excellent meal. Was this answer to prayer? Or maybe the neighbors just also got tired of the crowing. Who knows?

Is there a deep lesson to be learned from all this? Maybe just that a water pistol on the mission field is absolutely useless. But a good sense of humor will get you far.

A trip to the dentist

Adriaan, age 11, Mozambique

This week I had to go to the dentest. I live in Mozambique, and heer is no Dentest. The man just pulls all the teeth.

My dad took pictures of my teeth and sent it to the dentest in South Africa. He looked at the teeth and said they are baby teeth. Ok to pull. Thank you Dr. James. You are a better dentest.

Dad took me to another town, where the dentest is. It took the whole day to get there. My dad drove trhough a pothole as wide as the road. I almost bashed my head. My dad didn't swear. Promise. He is a Christian. Me too. We also went trhough more potholes but not so big.

This hospital is big and dirty and old. The doctor went to Cuba to learn how to help dentests. He loves Jesus. We waited for long before we could see him. He can't speak English, only Portugees. Now I know that "spit" in Portugees is "cuspier." And "does it hurt" is "doi" I know that "yes" is "Sim!" But all the other words are difficult, because he was speaking very fast. My sister understood some things.

Most of the tiles are not on the wall any more. Some old blood spatter on the tiles. The chair is old. Suddenly there was a big noise. My dad sed don't worry its only a compreser. He drilled my teeth. It was sore. He did not have enough anas ans anisthee anisthesia so he did not give me. Then I went the afternoon again. He drilled again. The drill is noisy. I hear lotsa people prayd for us. Maybe they thought he would drill through my cheek. He didn't. God heard. Thank you.

Now my teeth don't hurt any more. It is so nice. My dad bought me and my sister ice cream. In that city they have ice cream, not where we live.

Now we are back home. My dad knew where the biggest pothole was so he didn't have to not swear again.

Hee hee hee. Gotcha! Adriaan didn't write this, his dad did! Adriaan's Eenglish is much bettir.

Larger than life

Henry, Mozambique

Small-framed, joyful, artistic, and on the inside, stronger than strong. That's our daughter, Esté. When it comes to spiritual battles, she knows exactly who she is in Christ and the authority she carries.

We had been living in Mozambique for only six months when Esté, outgoing as she was, already had a large group of friends. One of them quickly became her closest friend. This girl confided in Esté about her scary nightmares and the feeling of a heavy, dark presence in her home. She told Esté she heard screams at night. Esté didn't hesitate. She knew the answer. The only complication? Her friend was a Muslim. But that did not deter Esté.

She explained to her friend the authority of Jesus, then walked boldly with her into that house and commanded the demons to leave. From that night on, her friend slept in peace. No more nightmares. No more fear. That's *my* Jesus!

Esté has always been adventurous. She and her friends would hitch rides on the back of open trucks going to the beach and back. These trucks had no rails at the back. It wasn't safe but she and her friends would hang onto each other, laughing all the way. Luckily, she only told us *years* after the fact. Yes, she is wise too...

God was looking out for her, giving her opportunities in a foreign land, a young girl who had been uprooted in her early teens from her familiar world in South Africa and from all her friends. Not long after our arrival, an orphanage in town, by divine timing, launched a dance outreach program. Esté and her friends eagerly joined. They poured hours into dance practice, rehearsals and performances, eventually being cast in a local production of *"The Lion King."*

One day, the man who led the training hit one of the kids with his fist. Esté saw that and when she said, "You shouldn't do that!," he replied, "The Bible says if someone hits you on one cheek, you should hit them on the other"...errr...*wait* a minute...

What we didn't know then was that this was how God was weaving these moments into His greater plan for Esté. The training, the joy of music and dance, the creativity, the fact that she was home-schooled... All of it prepared her for her next season of life. She was being trained for her future. A few years later, she enrolled in a Christian performing arts group back in South Africa, where, after some time, she met a cool-looking young American guy called Matt, who would later become her husband. And today she is an extraordinary mum who home-schools her two kids just like she was home-schooled, while following a career as an illustrator and artist.

God is the Master Planner. Every step, every encounter, every stage of life is a piece of His beautiful design.

CHAPTER FOUR

THE PROMISED LAND

Our "person of peace"

Henry, Mozambique

Where do we even begin to tell you about how the Lord opened the door to the Iso for us?

We stood on a hill overlooking the Iso village we believed God had sent us to, a large village of an estimated 10,000 people. To really engage with them, we had to, after a year of Portuguese studies, learn Iso next. Ten thousand people squashed together in mud huts along the beach— fiercely Muslim, tightly knit, wary of outsiders.

This village had a name made up of almost all the letters of the alphabet. Years later, a man we met in Singapore, insisted on wanting to know the name of the village. I explained to him that it was almost unpronounceable. Still, he insisted on hearing it. After I said the name, he went silent, thought for a moment, and then said, "Ah, *ParkingTicket!*" If you say it very fast, it nearly sounds the same.

People from the neighboring town had warned us some time before this: "Don't go walking around there. They'll kill you." We didn't quite believe that that would happen, but such comments, nevertheless, leave you slightly anxious. We knew God had really sent us there, so how could we take such advice and stay away? We were still living in a nearby town, but there was no time to waste. So we stood on that hill, praying for a while, and God was faithful. We both sensed we should go to a certain part of the village. So off we went— quickly, before our courage failed us.

We walked into a maze of huts and narrow sea-sand streets. The stares were intense—some wide-eyed with shock, some curious, others hostile. Many looked at us suspiciously. A little boy took one look at us and literally ran out of his pants in terror. He had never seen white people before.

Struggling to walk on the soft sea sand, we walked around a corner and suddenly we saw a woman sitting on her porch. The moment she saw us, she beamed. Her name was Amina. Like most Iso women, her Portuguese was halting, but with a combination of hand signs, a lot of laughter, Portuguese, and the little Iso we'd picked up, she understood that we wanted to learn her language. She eagerly invited us to come back to visit her. That moment was the beginning of a friendship that lasted for all the ten years we lived among the Iso.

Sometime later, we met her husband. He was a tailor who owned a small shop in the nearby town, though we didn't see him often. Months after we had finally moved into an ancient Portuguese-style house on the edge of *ParkingTicket*, he told us something that left us amazed: He was the sheikh[9]

9   In Islam, a sheikh is a man respected for his piety or religious

of the village, and the leader of the mosque just three houses away.

I was shocked, no, stunned. We both felt a twinge of anxiety. The sheikh? The religious leader? The man with influence over the whole village? But instead of being our enemy, he became a kind of protector. His friendship gave us legitimacy, respect, acceptance. Everyone knew the sheikh was our friend and ally—and that made all the difference.

Sometime after we learned this, I attended a marriage ceremony. In these ceremonies the men would sit in front of the house with the groom, and the women at the back with the bride. Many men had come from other villages. Unlike the locals, these outsiders didn't know me, or that we had become part of the community—loved, trusted, and accepted.

As I sat among the men, I began to sense a change in the atmosphere. Some of the men that came from other villages, started pointing at me, whispering to one another. I could see aggression spreading like a wave through the crowd as the whispering moved from person to person. The "whisper wave" was saying, "What is this white man doing here?" It occurred to me that if anything bad happened to me, no-one would ever know. I could simply vanish into thin air.

Eventually the whispering reached the sheikh and the other leaders who were sitting on a mat next to some incense that was burning, right beside a Quran. I watched closely. The sheikh leaned over to the person who had whispered something to him and calmly replied. I could see the other man's demeanor relaxing. This man then turned to speak to the one next to him, and just like the Chinese whispers game, the "whisper wave" gradually rolled back through the crowd

learning.

from where it came. Soon all signs of suspicion and hostility vanished. God had used the sheikh to protect me like a shield from fiery darts.

Another time, at a different ceremony, I was standing under the makeshift tent they had put up in the middle of the sea-sand street. A group of young, hostile men started surrounding me. They were insolent and their words threatening. Initially, I got a bit of a fright, but God helped me. I caught a glimpse of the sheikh who was standing not too far away, talking to another man. In a firm voice, I rebuked them for speaking so disrespectfully to me, an older man. By then, I understood their culture and how deeply they valued and respect older people.

I then turned around and walked slowly toward the sheikh, my back tingling all the way, half-expecting a physical attack from behind. But when I reached the sheikh, he greeted me warmly and introduced me to the other man he had been talking to.

When I glanced back out the corner of my eye, the aggressive young men had disappeared, dispersed in the crowd as if they had never been there. I still wonder today whether some of those young guys ended up in the militant Islamist insurgent group that later began to spread violence in the Iso area.

Once again, God had used the sheikh to keep me safe, turning what could have been a dangerous encounter into another reminder of His protection.

Think about this: How was it possible that we walked, almost directly, to the sheikh's house in a village of ten thousand people? Actually, it's very simple: When you step out in faith, trusting God, you can expect *God-incidences.*

"Whatever house you enter, begin by saying 'Peace to this house.' If a man of peace is there, your peace will rest on him; if not, it will return to you" (Luke 10:6). God had led us to *His* people of peace in the village.

Finding my identity

Henry, Mozambique

Before Mozambique, I used to be a businessman, working in the time-driven IT sector. Everything was done against the clock. Every new task that came in had to be done by yesterday. Suddenly, I now faced the opposite. What a contrast!

In Mozambique, tomorrow was another day, and everything was slow. You couldn't make it go faster. Many missionaries joke: "We have the watches; they have the time." But over the years, I learned to calm down. I learned to go with the flow. Slowly. Do you have to pay the account for water that comes in every two to three days? Then stand in line for three consecutive days to pay the bill. Fine. It's an opportunity to chat with people. I got to quite like the slow pace of life in the end.

In the beginning, it was quite an identity crisis for me. From a "self-made man," (yeah, right!), to a nobody living in the middle of nowhere and now with a low income. It took some getting used to. But it had been my choice, and I was fine with it.

My self-identity eventually changed from being a successful businessman to becoming a "tough" missionary, driving a four-wheel drive somewhere in Africa.

The "tough" missionary once broke down in tears in a fruit shop on a visit to South Africa. The day after we got back to South Africa, we went to the local fruit shop. Walking along the aisles and looking at all the colors, the flavors, the large selection of fruit in this huge shop caused vivid images of the lack we endured in Mozambique. There we had a few small bananas at the market, small onions, and wilted tomatoes. The contrast was just too overwhelming for me emotionally. I just sobbed.

My next identity change came after we moved to Asia. Gone was the four-wheel drive with the huge wheels. Driving the tiny car we'd bought, it felt as if we were skimming just above the road, dwarfed by towering trucks rumbling past our tiny car. Its little wheels looked no sturdier than thin cookies. When you got out of that car, you didn't climb down like with our four-wheel drive, you just got out. It felt very strange to me. This is difficult to explain if you haven't experienced it.

But the key through all of it was remembering my identity in Christ. I was, and still am, a friend of Jesus, beloved child of the Father. A new creation. The old has gone, the new has come. *That* is my true identity.

Salma's sweets

Betsy, Mozambique

Dressed in the local fashion with a headscarf and *kapulana*[10] cloth around my waist, carrying a big bag of roasted peanuts and brown sugar, I struggled through the narrow sea-sand streets to Salma's house. The obligatory, elaborate greetings and the usual questions of "Where are you going? What do

10   A type of a sarong worn primarily in Mozambique but also in other areas of Southeastern Africa.

you have there? What did you pay?" followed me all the way there. I didn't mind the constant repetition of the same phrases though; it's good for learning the language. Salma probably told everybody that I was coming because some of her neighbors stood waiting for me.

Today Salma was going to teach me to make a type of candy or "sweets," the local peanut brittle. For me, the visit was not really about learning how to make peanut brittle, but rather about making friends and learning more about Isoni and the local customs of the Iso. I knew this was going to be a tiring afternoon.

I had a year of Portuguese language studies behind me and had started learning Isoni. I knew a few basic words and some survival phrases, like: "Sorry, but I can't speak Isoni well." They would always reply, "But you just spoke Isoni!" Good point. A pity that was all I knew. Salma spoke Isoni and some other local languages of the area. The rest spoke only Isoni. They could all read Arabic. None spoke English. Henry always says the best English he ever heard there was when a little boy said to him, *"Hello, my seeester!*[11]*"* Contrary to the hopeful, but rather naive belief that everybody on the planet speaks English, there are many millions of people in this world who do not speak English at all. Not one word.

After replying to many greetings, the grandmother, Yaya, came out and sat on the ground. I had brought her some white sugar and tea bags as a gift. She took each tea bag and touched it as if it were a precious jewel. Then she touched her heart with an old, wrinkled hand and thanked me in Arabic.

Salma couldn't believe that I had bought the peanuts at one of the little stalls next to the road. She went off on a loud

11 Sister spoken with an accent.

rant in Isoni, of which I could understand only a smattering. Ignorance is bliss. Sometimes. Apparently, the peanuts at the road stall were much more expensive than buying them in bulk from some shop in the nearby town. I didn't know such a shop existed, but that was not the point. She repeated this apparent shocking news to the group of women standing there. They, too, laughed at my "stupidity."

Isoni Peanut Brittle 101: First, crush the peanuts in a flat basket, mainly to get the skins off. Salma then expertly took the basket and tossed the peanuts repeatedly into the air, using the basket to catch them again. This way the peanuts and skins separate. Amazing. I didn't know I had to learn that skill too, besides learning an undocumented tonal language so that I would be able to explain God's unconditional love and Jesus' sacrifice for sinners.

Talia, Salma's two-year-old daughter, had her hands in the basket all the time, and Granny Yaya would slap her on the head from time to time. Was that just a cultural expression of Iso-discipline or child abuse? I repeated the new-missionary mantra in my head: *It's not wrong, it's just different.* This is to help me not pre-judge people until I really know what's going on.

Next, the peanuts were thrown into a tall, wooden pot. Then came the pounding. Salma used a long, thick pole and smashed the peanuts repeatedly. Then I was given the pole and instantly I became the center of attention. Lord, I just wanted to tell people about Jesus, not become a food influencer. Everybody was watching me intently, laughing and pointing. Personally, I thought I was doing pretty well, that is until the *kapulana* around my waist started to loosen. Now I had to try to keep my *kapulana* up with one hand and pound at the same time. As soon as I stopped to try to adjust the *kapulana*, Salma yelled at me to go on. This was becoming quite stressful.

Granny came closely and watched me intently. Another neighbor came into the yard, and promptly she was also informed about the story about the expensive peanuts. Out of the blue, Granny poked me in the stomach and asked something in Isoni. Salma laughed and translated into Portuguese: "Why are you so fat? Do you have a baby in there?" I decided right there and then to give up on my diet, which was obviously not working.

After a lot of pounding, the peanuts had the same consistency as that of butter. While I was still pounding, Salma made a fire, put three stones on the ground and placed some firewood in the middle. One of the older kids went to the neighbor's house to fetch a few smoldering coals, carrying them in a dried-out coconut shell. How clever when you consider that there weren't any matches available! We put the pounded peanuts, brown sugar and some water in a pot on the fire and stirred it with a wooden stick.

While waiting for this mixture to do whatever it was supposed to do, I started thinking about the intelligence of the Iso chickens. These scrawny chickens were everywhere, wandering in each backyard of every house. They knew just how close to the stones and fire they could venture without a hot ember burning their feathers. Smart creatures. Suddenly, Yaya grabbed my sagging cloth and plucked it away from the fire. I didn't quite understand what she said to me, but I somehow don't think it was a compliment though.

A fishmonger came by, yelling at the gate. Salma's husband bought a few small fish from him for their evening meal and went back into the house. The fishmonger had also heard the whole story of the expensive peanuts. He just stood there, looking at me in utter amazement. How dumb can these foreigners be?

Meanwhile, the mixture on the fire had become a thick paste, like cookie dough, and Salma expertly threw it out onto a large, flat piece of wood. She pressed it down with a wooden stick, until it was spread out in a layer. After some time, it had cooled down a little so she could cut it into squares.

More waiting—and the squares became perfect pieces of peanut brittle. Not too bad for my first try at this! I never knew one could make peanut brittle in such basic circumstances. We were done for the day, and I was given four pieces to take home.... Really? After sponsoring the whole project, including the overpriced peanuts, spending a long afternoon in a cloud of confusion and smoke, I got only four pieces. Four!

I was still contemplating how I got cheated into getting only four measly little pieces when the call to prayer from the mosque made me realize that it was getting late. Dusk was approaching and I needed to get home. A lot of greetings followed as I left. My whole body ached. I had discovered muscles I never knew I had from pounding peanuts. The granny was still looking at me with a perplexed expression on her face as I struggled through their bamboo gate, my *kapulana* half-draped around my waist, burnt at the hem, and four very precious pieces of peanut brittle in my hand.

Yet I wanted to stay. I wanted to sit in the sand, with Talia on my lap, tugging at my arm hairs, while smelling the smoke of the fire and listening to the sizzle of frying fish. I wanted to eat coconut rice with my hands and listen for the hundredth time how friends and neighbors were entertained by the story of the dumb foreigner who bought the expensive peanuts.

When I had looked at Granny Yaya earlier, I realized that she was very, very old. I desperately wanted to tell her that Jesus was the Son of God and not just a good prophet, that He died for her so that she could have a home in heaven. Oh Lord, help me learn Isoni quickly.

To the weak I became weak, to win the weak. I have become all things to all people so that by all possible means I might save some (1 Corinthians 9:22).

Rafiki

Betsy, Mozambique

We were making steady progress learning Isoni. Every day I would go for a walk in the village, determined to speak with as many people as I could. Among our neighbors was a little three-year-old girl. She was terrified of me, perhaps because many in that community had never seen a white person before. Or maybe because the adults sometimes scared the kids by telling them that white people were vampires who would drink their blood if they weren't obedient. Whenever I visited, she would shrink back into a corner or hide behind her mother.

One afternoon, as I began my usual rounds, I stopped first at their house. Her mother sat outside, motionless. She looked exhausted and defeated. On her lap lay the little girl. At first glance I thought she was asleep, but as I came closer, my heart nearly stopped. This child looked gravely ill, unconscious even, her lifeless little body lying limp on her mother's lap.

The mother told me she had malaria. The hospital had sent them home. The medicine hadn't worked. The fever was so severe that the little girl had collapsed in her mother's arms, and now there was nothing more they could do.

I asked if I might pray for her, and she agreed without hesitation. My level of Isoni was still very basic. Yet I was so convinced that God is a God who heals, that, sometime before, I wrote out a simple prayer for healing in Portuguese and asked our language helper to translate it into Isoni so I could learn it by heart.

Looking back, it was perhaps not the wisest idea. I had no real vocabulary, no ability to explain or to follow up if God chose to work a miracle, or if people wanted to know more. But, if nothing else, give me credit for my passion.

I told her that I knew God could heal when we asked in the name of Jesus, and that I had seen Him do it before. When I finished praying, the little girl still looked lifeless. With nothing more to offer her, I continued on my way.

An hour or two later, on my way back home, I passed their house again. This time the mother was sitting alone. For a moment I froze, fearing the worst. Had the little girl died? With a heavy heart I walked toward her, silently praying for the right words to say.

But then she looked up at me with a big smile. "You didn't see her?," she asked. I was confused. Maybe I hadn't understood what she said. She pointed toward a group of children playing in a puddle in front of her house. And there she was, the same little girl, playing with the other kids in the water. I was stunned, overwhelmed, and deeply, deeply grateful. God had answered my prayer.

But He had done even more than saving this little girl's life. Her mother called her over, and instead of cowering as she always had, the little girl waddled straight toward me. She looked up at me and said a single word: "*Rafiki*." Best friend.

That's my God!

Loving the unlovable

Betsy, Mozambique

"You must love the Iso very much," people in South Africa commented while we were preparing to move to the Iso. Well, to be honest, in the beginning we didn't. We hadn't even *met* any of them before moving there! How could we love people who were faceless, voiceless—only a name on a list of Unreached People Groups?

Yet we came to live among the Iso people, being the only foreigners in a village of ten thousand Iso. We were treated with suspicion at first. They confessed to us much later that some of the adults disciplined their children by telling them that we were vampires! They thought it was hilarious.

Even though we were seen as vampires by some, we persevered in being sincerely friendly. And making the most ridiculous mistakes—unintentionally—when speaking Isoni, helped to dissolve their suspicions.

Gradually, the Iso got used to us. We got used to them. But love? The Lord brought that, too. I quickly made many friends.

Except for one.

Ani was my neighbor. And a very annoying one, too, it turned out. She was rude, unfriendly, brash, demanding, unkind—even cruel. Any other negative adjectives out there? She was all of them. She would come to our house often, sometimes three times a day, either to gossip about people or to demand things.

One time I gave her a pumpkin, because she said she was hungry. Her response was not "Thank you," but rather, "Where's the sugar and oil? How do you expect me to cook this without sugar and oil?" I duly delivered the sugar and oil.

At other times, she would come over and order me to take her, together with her harvested rice, over to the mill. It was like she owned me. Many times she would just laugh mockingly in my face when I didn't understand what she was saying, or when I did not understand the Iso customs. That was not nice of her. I often asked God to change her. Now I know, depicting her like this, makes me seem to be a saint in contrast, right?

I just could not get to the point where I liked Ani. It eventually started to bother me. Here we were, coming all the way from South Africa, giving up our business, sacrificing a life of easy comforts (yeah, I knew I would receive my rewards someday), in the sincere motivation to come and tell the Iso about Jesus and His love for them. How then could I not even love my closest neighbor? In my defense, nobody in the village liked Ani. She was quite infamous.

Love your enemies, do good to those who hate you, bless those who curse you, pray for those who mistreat you (Luke 6:27-31).

I started praying earnestly about this—which I should have done from the start—asking, no begging, the Lord to help me. I told God how I tried to love her, just in case He didn't know about it. I told Him how I constantly went over with gifts and tried to share Bible stories with her, so she could change. And I confessed to God that I really, really did not like her. I came to the end of my rope and realized that it would take a miracle for me to love her. Finally I prayed, asking God to help me love Ani with the love *He* had for her.

I had been praying like this for a few weeks, when Ani came to the house one day for her daily gossip session. We sat outside in the shade while she informed me of the latest happenings in the village.

Suddenly, while she was talking, it was as if I became deaf. I could see her mouth moving but could not hear a word. Initially, I found it quite amusing. Ah, bliss. Silence *is* golden. But in that silence, while looking at her moving mouth, God poured *His* love for Ani all over me, like someone pouring a bucket of water over my head. It was an intense experience. I was quite overcome with emotion. In that instant, I saw her in a completely different light. She was strong, resilient, she loved her family above everything, and she was creative in finding food resources. In that moment I realized how much I respected her, yes loved her. After a few minutes of having these intense emotions, my hearing slowly returned. Shortly after, she went home. I was in a daze for the rest of the day.

From then on, our friendship blossomed. And then Ani began to change. She became grateful, considerate and friendly. God responded to my prayers, right? Which one? The one to change her, or the one to help me to love her? He changed *my* heart first! I realized that she had noticed when I started treating her differently, and by showing her respect, love and acceptance, not dutiful neighborly tolerance, she responded to that love by becoming lovable too.

I saw her no longer as a project, but as a person, made in the image of God, a daughter of the King.

When God sent the wind

Henry, Mozambique

The Iso boats are called "dhows." They look ancient, like the pictures of the boats Jesus and His disciples used. They have no motors—only sails that have been patched a thousand times. And they leak like sieves, so someone has to bail water constantly. These *dhows* are made of wood and have large triangular sails made of pieces of cloth sewn together. No gasoline is required; you just need the wind. Perfect.

Until there was no wind.

We had been sitting in a *dhow* for hours on the open sea. It was hot. There was no wind. The only sound you could hear was the creaking of the boat floating on the water.

I was on the boat with two missionaries from another town and some Iso Muslim men. We were headed to an island where more Iso people lived. Between us, we had enough Isoni to hold real conversations. This was an opportunity that was too good to waste. So, we talked. We told stories about Jesus, stories about life, then about the weather. Still no wind. Back to the topic of Jesus again. This went on for hours.

Finally, one of us said, "We're going to pray that God will send a wind." They scoffed and laughed at us. To them, God was too high above, far away, remote, unreachable. We prayed anyway. Nothing. They laughed, shaking their heads. We prayed again.

A breeze began to flutter the sail ever so slightly, just enough to fill it. And we were on our way. No laughing anymore. Just silence. And then the slight whooshing sound of the wind playing with the sails. The seeds of faith had been sown.

Jesus Christ is the same yesterday and today and forever (Hebrews 13:8).

Insiders and outsiders

Betsy, Mozambique

I would visit a family almost every day to listen, observe, and stumble my way through new Isoni words. This family baked bread for a living, and I would often "help" them. They quickly discovered that I was hopeless at braiding dough. My clumsy fingers tied knots worthy of a sailor, not a baker. Between my tangled "braids" and tangled Iso sentences, there was plenty of laughter at my expense. But they loved me anyway: for dressing like them, eating with my hands like them, and for bravely butchering their language.

Before I go on, I need to explain something about the Iso. Most of them live right on the beach in small mud huts, fishing for their livelihood. They are poor. Very poor. They have no toilets because it is not possible to dig proper holes in loose sea sand. So, what do you do when nature calls? You answer it right there on the beach.

Now, don't imagine crashing waves sweeping everything away. Oh no. The sea is just a gentle lap. Which means... yes, "it" all stays there, decorating the sand and rocks, if you will. And if you want to get to your little fishing boat, you tiptoe through a minefield unlike any other.

One afternoon, while we were baking and chatting, a child shouted for us to come quickly to the bamboo fence that separated the house from the beach. Dutifully, like any good Iso, I joined the crowd, peering through the slats to see what the excitement was about.

And there they were, a couple walking along *that* beach. Shorts, caps, fanny packs, sunglasses, water bottles. The full tourist uniform. They obviously came from the nearby town because nobody would visit *ParkingTicket* for fun.

A lively debate broke out. "Those white people must be lost," one said. "No, no, they're searching for something," another suggested. Everyone was speculating as to why those white strangers would be walking there. Not a single person mentioned the obvious. I was white too.

In that moment, I wasn't an outsider anymore. To them, I wasn't one of *those* white strangers. I was *their* white Iso—the oddball who dressed like them, ate their food, and shared their laughter. On that day, the line was clearly drawn. There were the Iso, who knew the perils of the beach and there were the clueless tourists.

And I knew exactly which side of the fence I belonged to.

A typical day in *ParkingTicket*

Henry, Mozambique

Over the years, many people have asked us, "So, what do you do every day?" There's really no simple answer—except maybe, "it depends." Our routines shifted depending on the season we were in: language learning and chronological story translations, evangelism, doing recordings, or discipling the new believers. But I'll try to describe a typical day during our language learning phase—if there ever was such a thing.

We wake up at 4 a.m., when the sun rises. By then, the sweat from my head has already soaked through my pillow and into the mattress. That's just life in the tropics—no air conditioning, no fans, no relief from the sweltering heat. We get up, spend an hour or so with the Lord, then have breakfast with the kids.

At 7 a.m. sharp, Betsy and the children begin with home-schooling, and I set off for my language session with Zuba, my language helper, whose house is about a ten-minute walk away. But it's never just a simple walk to get to his house. The narrow sea-sand streets are packed with people to greet. And you must greet everyone.

At Zuba's house, I record phrases in Isoni for an hour or two. When I get back home, I upload the recordings to the computer and play them back to practice—training my ear rather than my eyes. I log new words onto a spreadsheet that doubles as our dictionary. During her coffee break, Betsy practices the same words, and later in the afternoon we visit friends to use what we've learned.

Betsy cooks everything from scratch. Lunch would be Portuguese bread, called *Pão*. Most nights we have rice and beans. Sounds easy, right? Not exactly. First the beans have to be sorted—one by one—because nobody likes the surprise of biting into a small stone. The rice gets the same treatment. Then it is the tomatoes' turn, which are carefully evaluated and separated into two piles: the "proud and presentable" tomatoes for salad, and the "soft, slightly defeated" tomatoes for stews. Only after all this does the actual cooking begin.

And, of course, that's usually when life decides to interrupt—as it often does.

Someone shows up at our door: "So-and-so just died. Please come to the funeral." In Islam, the dead must be buried within 24 hours. So off we go, walking to their house under the blazing sun. The men gather at the front of the house, the women at the back. I sit on the southern edge of the crowd, careful that when they bow toward Mecca, no one notices that I stay seated, cross-legged, quietly praying in my own way. By the time we return home, we're drenched in sweat. The kids have been finishing their schoolwork while we were gone.

In the evenings, we just hang out with the kids, waiting for the air to cool down. We sleep in the "school room" on the floor on mattresses when there is no electricity, which happens often, because that room has no windows, only mosquito netting. It was the only place where the air moved a little to give us some relief from the heat.

Around 1 or 2 a.m., pounding on the door jolts us awake —again. Someone is about to give birth, and they need "the ambulance." Our car, the only vehicle in a village of ten thousand, is it. I'm slow to wake up, so Betsy takes the wheel. I help load everyone in—not just the expectant mother, but her extended family too. Some have never been in a car before; they sit on their haunches on the seats, unsure what to do. After delivering them safely to the clinic in the nearby town, we drive home. The clinic was about five km (three miles) from home. Now I'm wide awake. The day is about to begin.

Besides going to my language helper, this morning's task is paying the water and electricity bills. We receive water every second day, if we're lucky, and electricity for three to six hours a day—and yet the bills still come. I pray it won't take three days to pay the bills like last month. At the office, also in the nearby town, you stand in a long queue, together with everyone else trying to pay, and slowly inch your way forward... By the time you get to the cubicle, it's too late. They are closing for the day, or they have run out of change. Come back tomorrow. Hard to believe, but that's how it is. However, today is a good day and I get off easy—it only took three hours.

When I get home, Betsy is off to the market...

Rice and beans

Betsy, Mozambique

Life in *ParkingTicket*, with its coconut-and-onion markets, second-hand clothes for sale set up in bamboo stalls next to the road, and a slower pace for everything, means life was simple, which sounds idyllic, only if you are living that simple life for real. Living in a sun-scorched, mosquito-infested village was not a walk in the park.

Getting food for the family was a real challenge. Money wasn't the problem—the food was. Or rather, the lack of it. My weekly trips to the market in the nearby town became prayer journeys. First, I prayed I wouldn't get stopped by the traffic police; they had a habit of preying on single women. After a few unpleasant encounters, Henry started coming with me.

Then I'd pray that my favorite vendor was there. Shopping for food was all about relationships. I eventually learned to stick with one guy—his prices were inflated, but at least they were consistently inflated. He was my guy and I would only buy from him. Sometimes I'd arrive at the market and find nothing. Absolutely nothing. That's when I realized I'd forgotten to pray that there would be food at the market.

From there, I had to drive to another market to buy beans and rice—sold in huge heaps beside a dirt road. Again, I went to the same man every time. He'd measure out the rice and beans with an old tin can.

Back home, I'd spend time picking out small stones from the beans before cooking them. I learned to bake bread using soft peanut skins as "bran," and even made my own yogurt. Everything was done from scratch.

Coming up with interesting meals when the choice of food was limited, was one of my biggest challenges. Our daughter Esté, always the comedian, once helped me to plan the menu for the week's meals. It was difficult, but we managed to come up with the following:

Monday—Beans-and-rice and papaya.

Tuesday—Sloppy Joes made of leftover beans on a locally made bread roll, and papaya.

Wednesday—Beans-and-tomato stew, coconut rice, and papaya.

Thursday—Beans-and-rice, and bananas.

Friday—Fried rice with beans, and bananas.

Saturday—Beans and egg frittata.

When we came to Sunday, we were stumped. We needed something special and interesting. Then Esté came up with the following hilarious concept:

Sunday—Bean surprise!

We laughed at all our bean jokes, bean meals, and bean surprises. If all else fails, smile …

One time, we saw an ad for a newly opened café at a rustic hotel across the bay. The sign read: "Cuisine theme: Where Africa meets Asia." This gave us quite a laugh. We wondered if you could eat beans with chopsticks there.

Just a heads-up here. If you do not have a sense of humor, get one before you live cross-culturally. You will need it. Somehow, smiling relieves the tension. The Lord also has a sense of humor—I'm sure of it. Why else would He give us one?

Fly with us!

Henry, Africa

The following newsletter about one of our five-day return trips, after a resupply run to South Africa, somehow landed at a missionary aviation ministry. This ministry was so entertained (and a little horrified) that they asked us if they could use our newsletter as an advertisement to convince people to fly with them, instead of driving that road!

Here's the newsletter. Decide for yourself whether it was a good choice for an advertisement.

To describe the trip back to *ParkingTicket* as a nightmare might be overstating it. But then again, it might not. Because it was the rainy season and the road was muddy, we decided to cut through the small country of Malawi where we knew the roads were better.

All went well until the third day when disaster struck, while we were in the middle of nowhere. We had just bounced through some bad potholes when our fully laden trailer's left wheel broke off and disappeared into the bush. The last village we had passed through was probably about 200 km back (120 miles), and the next town was about 90 km ahead

(60 miles) of us. Even though things looked pretty hopeless at the time, a supernatural peace fell upon all of us.

We had just decided to pack as much stuff as possible into the car and leave the trailer there to seek help when a man on a motorbike came by and offered to help. It turned out he was a mechanic from an unmapped small village a few miles ahead. Wonderful. Fortunately, we had an extra set of wheel bearings with us. After a good three hours of battling the hi-lift jack and various bits and pieces, we were on the road again, but now without a brake on the left side of the trailer. We spent the night in a town on the way to the border with Malawi.

After crossing the border, we planned to sleep only one night in Malawi and to cross back into Mozambique the day after. In Malawi, along a slippery, muddy road, about 6 km (4 miles) from the place we were planning to stay, the wheel broke off again. It was pouring down with rain. This time we did not have any spare parts left, and again we were stuck in the middle of nowhere. This time we did not have the peace we felt the first time it happened.

Everything went wrong at the same time. It was a Saturday afternoon and we only had a small amount of Malawian currency with us, with no possibility of changing more until the next Monday. To make things even worse, our transit visas expired on that same Monday.

After managing to unhitch the trailer, Esté and I went looking for a mechanic. I left Betsy and Adriaan behind to guard the trailer while we were gone. After much searching, we found a mechanic, and after much negotiation, another man who reluctantly agreed to guard the trailer until we could get it fixed. (Nobody wants to be a guard in the pouring rain.)

We then returned to find Betsy and Adriaan standing next to the road, soaked and miserable.

Betsy

I was fuming! Judge me now or never, but I was mad at God. I felt like citing David over and over again: "Wake up, O Lord! Why are You sleeping?" (Psalm 44). "Why have you forgotten us? How long must we struggle? How long will the devil pester us until you come to the rescue?" (Psalm 13 and 22). I was done. I just couldn't handle this anymore. Behaving much like a stubborn teenager, I told God I won't talk to Him again until He helps us.

Henry

We found a place nearby that rented out rooms and decided to stay there for the night. We unpacked everything that was in the car and carried it into the room. The next day, we could fetch more belongings from the trailer and leave them in the room too. We weren't sure exactly how reliable our newly found guard would be. And we had brought a year's supply of provisions, items we couldn't buy in northern Mozambique, like school books, medicine and even milk powder.

The room was filthy and there was only cold water available in the bathroom. We managed to sleep in the end, despite the fact that the pillows (without pillowcases) smelled of the many unwashed heads of numerous previous occupants. I was the only one who was willing to dare take a cold shower, wearing my sandals, because the shower floor was so dirty. If this place were to be rated, it would have been a *negative* five-star hotel.

The next day we went to fetch the mechanic and got him working on fixing the trailer. While he was busy, we unpacked more supplies from the trailer into the car and set off for our hotel. But while we had been away, the river flowing down the mountain right next to the village, had overflowed. The last bridge to our hotel was now under water. There was no way through. We spent that night at another hotel called the *Chididi Motel*. The slogan outside read: "Your away second home."

The mechanic turned out to be an angel. We didn't have any Malawian currency to pay for the room and this man even lent us money for that. Remember, no credit cards here.

Unfortunately, all our toiletries, towels, food, etc. were still at the other hotel! Looking as though we'd just been for a dip in the pool, with our clothes on, we took cold showers and dried ourselves with Adriaan's T-shirt. There were no towels at our "away second home." The next morning we had cheese and chocolate for breakfast from our small fridge in the car, because all our other food was either in the trailer or at the first hotel across from the flooded river. The day after, we were able to fetch rusks (South African biscotti) from the trailer. And what a feast that was.

Only two long days later were we able to get through and over the bridge, to fetch the supplies we had left in the room.

The next problem we faced was that our transit visas were only valid for three days. They were expiring on that very day. We drove east for half an hour, toward the border. At the border post they told us they could not extend our visas. For that, we had to go to Blantyre city, which is an hour and a half's drive in the other direction. Off we went.

We entered the immigration office, thinking that this would be a mere formality. There were two immigration officials behind the counter and one of them was busy. We walked over to the other official and explained our situation, who then said, "Oh, big problem. Big problem. Not easy." At that stage we didn't yet know that his words were actually code for asking for a bribe. After some arguing back and forth, we finally came to realize that this guy wasn't going to extend our visas without a bribe.

We prayed silently for the Lord to make a way. At that exact moment, the office phone rang. Our designated official was called to the phone in the room next door. When the man got up and went to take the call, the other official came up to us and asked us if he could help. A thought from the Lord flashed through my mind, and I said "The other man was busy extending our visas." He looked at the documents, saw that there was no problem, and stamped our passports. As we rushed out the door, I saw that our original official's call had ended. He half-lifted his hand to stop us, but we were already out the door. With our stamped passports. Praise the Lord. What exact timing. Yet another "*God-incidence.*"

The rest of the day we spent in Blantyre searching for the spare parts in the sprawling markets and arranging for the welding of the wheel. As it turned out, the workshop's electricity supply was being repaired, and we could only fetch the wheel two days later. Two more days at the *Chididi Motel.* That day we also managed to find a pay telephone from where we could make an international call to inform Charles, the coordinator of our core support team, of our dilemma, and we also managed to change some money for Malawian currency.

Betsy

I relented and "forgave" God for not hearing us, for not helping us. Things were starting to look better. There was hope that we would eventually get back to *ParkingTicket*. It was like the sun starting to shine through black, big clouds. And I was *so* relieved to be talking to God again.

Henry

Two days later we returned to Blantyre, fetched the newly welded wheel, and the mechanic finished fixing the trailer. The very next day we reached a dreaded border post, infamous for its greedy officials just looking to find fault in order to demand bribes. We were very relieved when they let us through, but only after they searched the entire trailer. And then we were back in Mozambique. The road we feared might be impassable, turned out to be not too bad. Traveling 180 km (110 miles) in five hours, all the while watching the wobbling trailer wheel closely in the mirror and stopping to inspect it every 50 km (31 miles) or so was reasonably acceptable. When we reached a well-known mission station, we took the wheel off again, tightened the nut more, and spent the night there. A great relief.

The next day everything went fine until we reached a little dump (oops, I mean town) next to the road. As we were leaving the town, people waved furiously at us. I checked the trailer's wheel in the rear-view mirror, saw that it was not wobbling unduly, so we carried on. Suddenly we reached a universal informal traffic warning sign in Africa—branches across the road. We looked ahead and saw a huge, gaping hole where the bridge used to be. That's why we never traveled at night. The bridge was no more and there was no way of crossing that chasm. We had to go back into the town and try to find an alternative route, which we managed to do. The diversion meant we had to drive very slowly, between five and twenty km/h (three to twelve mph). It took us two hours to get back to the main road again.

When we had driven down the same main road, about a month before, it was an average quality dirt road where we could do between seventy and eighty km/h (fifty mph). During that one month, it had degraded so much that we doubted that we were actually driving on the same road. Praise the Lord that we didn't have the downpour we'd had in Malawi. We were grateful that the weather was fine and the roads were not muddy.

Our final bit of excitement came when we discovered, at around midday, that the rear bumper on which the tow bar was mounted, had come loose on one side and was almost dragging on the ground. Two bolts had vibrated loose. I had to jack up the trailer in order to bend the tow bar back into position, and screw two new bolts in.

Eventually we made it back to *ParkingTicket* with everything intact, but our nerves. The trailer wheel drum and brakes still had to be replaced, though.

What did this trip mean to us as a family? Well, once again, our children amazed us with their perseverance and inner strength. I remember watching Adriaan bravely guarding his mother and the trailer in the pouring rain as we drove away looking for help. A pillar of strength at eleven years of age. Only once were they in tears, and I couldn't blame them. I came pretty close myself. Our children have really matured spiritually through experiencing these kinds of trials, and we praise the Lord for this.

If you've read the account of our trials and tribulations thus far, you deserve to hear of the spiritual side of things. This is not intended to be a theological treatise on "Why God allows suffering," just some of my thoughts and observations during this trip.

Why does God allow these kinds of trials? We prayed for protection a lot, and many people were also praying for us, although they didn't know about our predicaments until they were almost over.

There are many viewpoints on prayer: how to pray, what you can pray for, etc. Well, we prayed in all the ways we know how, yet events still worked out as they did. Some Christians suggested that we might have been out of the will of God because He allowed such hardships. Even though we are very far from being perfect, we believe that anyone involved in missions, (going to the mission field, praying, or supporting) is within the published will of God, as stated in the Great Commission in Matthew 28:18-20.

Often such trials happen because God is maturing us spiritually. That is true, for we all do need spiritual maturity. You'll often hear Christians say that He will never test you beyond your ability to endure. But look what Paul said about this in 2 Corinthians 1:8,

"We were under great pressure, far beyond our ability to endure."

Perhaps they're thinking of 1 Corinthians 10:13, "... *He will not let you be **tempted** beyond what you can bear."*

Temptation and hardships are two very different things. Fortunately, He did help us to endure, and He built us up in the process. As I was trying to make sense of what was happening to us, this verse came to mind where Jesus said to Peter in Luke 22:31-32,

"Simon, Simon, Satan has asked to sift you as wheat. But I have prayed for you, Simon, that your faith may not fail. And when you have turned back, strengthen your brothers."

This reminded me that we are in a spiritual battle.

"For our struggle is not against flesh and blood, but against the rulers, against the authorities, against the powers of this dark world and against the spiritual forces of evil in the heavenly realms" (Ephesians 6:12).

At one point during the ordeal, it felt as if we were physically being kept out of Mozambique. Everything seemed to be conspiring to keep us out. Once we were able to phone our core support team leader, more people started praying for us. Then everything started working out right in our favor. This served to remind us that we are part of a larger team, namely our missions agency, all who volunteer to pray for us, and those who support us financially. Missionaries can't do the work without support. It is the Lord that makes things happen, but He wants to involve all of us Christians in His greater plan.

Even though salvation is God's free gift, we tend to forget that Jesus also said there would be a price to pay:

"And whoever does not carry his cross and follow Me cannot be My disciple. Which one of you, wishing to build a tower, does not first sit down and count the cost..." (Luke 14:27).

Jesus Himself made shocking statements. Read Luke 14:26-33 and Matthew 10:37-38.

John MacArthur wrote this:

"Salvation is absolutely free. So is joining the army. You don't have to buy your way in. Everything you

need is provided. But there is a sense in which following Christ—like joining the army—will cost you dearly. It can cost freedom, family, friends, autonomy, and possibly even your life." (John MacArthur, *The Gospel According to the Apostles*).

Experiences like these have a way of sending you back to the book of Job.

We praised the Lord for being faithful. We knew He was with us always, even to the end of the age. We knew He was real, and that He loved us. He carried us through all these misadventures and would surely carry us through whatever lay ahead. He was, and is, amazing and faithful. He doesn't always keep us from bad situations, but He goes through them with us, for the sake of growing our faith (Psalm 23).

You prayed big

Betsy, Mozambique

My friend Amina, the sheikh's wife, and I had struck up a friendship from the very beginning. Spending time in her home each day, I learned that her baby niece was gravely ill. In desperation, the family finally took the child to the "hospital" in the nearby town. I use quotation marks deliberately, because what passed for a hospital was something out of a war zone. Some wards had no running water. There were no proper doctors. Families had to provide food for their loved ones who stayed there. It was filthy, crumbling and overrun with disease.

When I heard that the baby had been taken there, my first thought was that she would not survive that hospital. I took Amina and some of her family members to the hospital. As we entered the ward, I was struck by the sight: beds crammed together with scarcely enough space to walk between them, each holding a sick patient surrounded by anxious relatives. The smell of sickness, blood and vomit was overwhelming. Cholera here, malaria there, and other unnamed illnesses and diseases everywhere.

I knew I had to pray for that child, but at that moment I realized every single person there was Muslim. That, I admit, was intimidating. Yet my compassion for this tiny baby outweighed my fear. I whispered a silent prayer for courage, then haltingly asked in broken Isoni if I could pray for the baby. To my surprise, they welcomed it eagerly.

I prayed the one prayer I had memorized—asking God to heal. The prayer was short and simple, one that I learned by heart, because my Isoni was not yet at a level that allowed me to pray freely. It felt a little awkward since none of them had ever seen a Christian pray before, much less pray for healing. Nothing dramatic happened. We left the hospital quietly.

But Henry and I carried that baby in our prayers the rest of the day. The next morning, as I walked toward Amina's house, she joyously came running out to meet me, her face shining. "You prayed *big!*" she exclaimed. The baby had been released from the hospital the previous evening.

I wish I could have explained more clearly that it wasn't my big prayer, but a big God who had answered. My language wasn't sufficient, but the lesson was clear: God's power is not limited by my words.

CHAPTER FIVE

DYING TO SELF

Spiritual act of worship

Betsy, Mozambique

The scarf over my hair kept sliding off as I walked, trying awkwardly to keep the tight cloth in place around my waist. The sand was hot and soft, which made walking even more difficult.

What happened to that quiet librarian sitting at her desk, organizing books, subject by subject? I even had the glasses to complete the stereotype.

This was my second outing of the day. I had forgotten to wear a headscarf earlier that morning, and as soon as I passed the neighbor's house, the old grandmother sitting outside sternly told me to go back and "dress properly." Apparently, I was shaming my husband. I had found out the hard way that walking down the street in *ParkingTicket* without a headscarf was immodest.

However, I felt really pleased with myself. There was great progress in my language learning. It took me a long time to walk through the village to Amina's house. She was my self-appointed language teacher. She made me write out all the new words she gave me. She could only read Arabic, so it didn't matter what I wrote—but I wrote them down dutifully. Her little girl, Lila, sat on my lap, pulling at the hairs on my arm. I learned the word for "arm hairs": *malaika*. A very important word to know.

It was hot. I was soaking wet with perspiration. I could smell myself.

Amina's husband was on his way to the mosque and gave me his elbow to shake, not his hand. He was the sheikh and had just washed so he could go to the mosque to pray. He couldn't touch me now. How do you shake an elbow? I was not out of my comfort zone here—there was *no* comfort zone near!

I really needed to go home. I was exhausted, but also felt elated. Satisfied. Thanks, Lord!

Everyday followed almost the same routine: visiting people, making friends, learning new words. Many people asked me for money. Should I give to them? And if I did, how much? If I gave to everyone that asked, we would run out of funds within ten minutes. I got stuck at a house where the grandmother was lying in the shade of her grass-roofed hut. She had malaria. I offered to pray and prayed the prayer I had learned by heart. God knew my heart.

At another house a few Iso men and women were playing a board game. They insisted that I play with them. I had no idea how to play or what was happening. I just knew that I had lost the game—to the great delight of the whole group of spectators. I was really dying to myself, my pride, my desire to be in control.

That day, on the way home, I passed a few women on their way to their small rice farms, just outside of the village. It was always a big trip for them to get there. They too asked for money. I asked if I could pray for them. I prayed that God would send His angels to protect them. I got very strange looks.

By now, I was sort of getting used to the incessant sweating. Nevertheless, I felt so content. How was this possible? It was really difficult living there. My comfort zone had been annihilated. I was learning to bake bread, learning to pray in Isoni, learning how to love people in an undocumented language. Thank you Lord for making that easy for me.

I got the feeling God was surprised at me for not knowing why I was so content in such a strange and comfort zone-less surroundings.

Don't you know this is your act of worship? You are worshiping Me, He said in my spirit.

I was stunned. I never thought that God saw my feeble attempts to love the Iso as worship. That changed my attitude toward sitting and waiting for hours in the hot sun at funerals. And taking women in labor to the clinic at two o' clock in the morning. Or eating the small fried fish with their eyes still intact, staring at me, because my Iso friends cooked them, my friends who did not know that Jesus loved them more than I could ever do.

I eventually learned why the women had looked at me so strangely when I prayed that God would send His angels to protect them. This beautiful Iso language that God had created is tonal, and I was mixing up the words for "arm hairs" (*malaika*) and "angels" (*malaa-ika*). I suppose God could use His arm hairs to protect us, right?

Malaria

Henry, Mozambique

Disclaimer / Parental Caution PG-13: Do not read on if you are easily upset by the reality of medical emergencies.

People have often asked us if we ever got malaria in Mozambique. Of course, yes, we did. "How many times?" Well, about ten times, each one of us. "But didn't you take preventative medicine?" "Yes, we did, but one can't take prophylaxis (preventative medicine for malaria) over the long term." We also added to this, "We've found that when we take prophylaxis, we get malaria about once a year. When we don't take it, we get malaria about once every twelve months." Work it out. That's why we stopped taking it.

Some people have asked us what it is like to have malaria. Is it like having a cold or the flu? Did you really have malaria, or perhaps just a bad flu? Is it really life-threatening? So, I decided to write a report about a malaria attack directly after recovering from a bout of malaria, and before the memory faded.

Malaria seems to attack the body differently every time, making it difficult to describe the symptoms precisely. For that reason, I will now describe one specific bout of malaria as it happened:

Wednesday: I feel a bit flu-ish, and a bit "off." I drink some vitamin C and flu/cold pills. Doesn't help. I carry on with my work as usual.

Thursday: Feeling the same as yesterday. My body is aching a bit. I carry on working. I wonder if perhaps there is a bout of malaria coming, but I doubt it because I had malaria just two weeks ago.

Friday morning: I get up and feel as if I have a bad flu, my body is aching, I have a headache, I feel tired. Betsy suggests I cancel my appointment for recording Scripture today, which I gratefully do. Computer work is not as tiring, so I write a report for World Outreach that is due and send it out. Around 9:30 I feel it would be better if I just got into bed.

Suddenly, I am too weak to stand or even sit. My body is aching so much that I don't want to lie down. Any contact with the bed hurts terribly. It is not too hot in the house, "only" 36°C (98°F), yet I start shaking uncontrollably from cold shivers. Betsy fetches the malaria test kit. When she draws blood to test, I hardly feel the pin prick on my fingertip, as it hurts much less than the rest of my body. The kit indicates three lines immediately. It is malaria without a doubt. Betsy prays for me.

The malaria parasites which had entered my body when the female Anopheles mosquito bit me, had been multiplying in my liver for two weeks. Once ready, they were released into my bloodstream, making their home in my red blood cells. As they grow in the blood cells, the red blood cells burst. This causes blood infection. Every twelve hours, the parasite count doubles. My blood can no longer carry enough oxygen to my body tissues. The body tissues are asphyxiating, causing great pain. It is strange that I could still recall Scripture during all of this: "The life of the creature is in the blood." While writing this down later, I found it in Leviticus 17:11.

My body is fighting for survival. A missionary colleague recently asked me: "Do you also feel that you're dying each time you have malaria?" Yes, I do. I know that if something doesn't stop the malaria, I will become part of the statistics, just another victim of this dreadful disease.

Malaria is still one of the biggest killers in Africa. Far more people die every year from malaria than from AIDS. But right now, I am too sick to think about this. To attack the malaria parasites in my body, Betsy gives me *Artemisinin* and *Doxycycline* immediately. I shake so much that I can hardly hold the glass of water I need to take the tablets with. Despite the heat, Betsy has to heap all the blankets we have on me. I shake and shiver to such an extent that my teeth clatter. Betsy and I try to praise the Lord. He is the same under all circumstances. It sounds pretty pathetic, though. But we know He is with us, always. My head hurts something awful.

I can't get warm. Betsy gets into bed with me and lies on top of me to warm me up. She perspires; I shiver and shake. After some time, she can't take the heat anymore and must get off the bed. Eventually the shaking stops and I start breathing normally again.

My muscles ache from the violence of the shaking. I realize that I have muscles in places that I didn't know I had. Gradually my body temperature starts to rise. Higher and higher. I throw off the blankets one by one. Betsy is standing by the whole time. I can scarcely turn around in bed by myself.

I start perspiring. After a few minutes, I lie in a pool of perspiration. There are now two fans blowing on me. I have a splitting headache. There is no possibility of sleep. I am exhausted. I can't eat, even though I'm hungry. I try to take in as much water as I can, because I know dehydration is a danger.

Betsy sends a text message to our prayer coordinator in South Africa to ask that people pray for me. We only do this in emergencies We don't want to "cry wolf" every time something goes wrong.

My temperature reaches 40.8°C (105°F). Betsy helps me to the shower. I initially open it so that only drops come out (we don't have hot water). The water feels like ice crystals. It hurts, but I persevere until I get used to the cold. Then I open it up some more. I struggle to remain standing in the shower. I hold onto Betsy. After a while my temperature gets under control and she helps me back to bed. My body hurts.

Arie, the doctor at the nearby Leprosy Mission, comes to see how I'm doing. I see him calling Betsy to one side. She told me afterward he said that if I didn't improve soon, I'll have to be evacuated. He suggests we use stronger medicine, *Coartem,* in combination with *Fansidar*, which is another type of malaria treatment. He suspects there is resistance to the medicine I have been taking.

It's five o'clock and time for my medication again. I can't keep any food down, so I'm taking it on an empty stomach. I feel nauseous but I know that if I vomit the tablets out, I am in big trouble. Betsy keeps an eye on the clock, waiting for an hour to pass. I manage to keep the medicine down.

I hardly sleep at all, intermittently drifting in and out of sleep. Betsy doesn't sleep at all. She prays all the time. When I become too quiet, she touches me to check if I am still breathing. My temperature peaks again at 39.8°C (104°F). I feel the fan blowing too strongly on me. Eventually I manage to sit up to change it to a slower speed. Thankfully, the electricity stays on. After a while I notice that the fan is still running at the same speed. I realize that in my delirium I had only *imagined* getting up and setting it slower. I drift in and out of consciousness all night. I am so very tired.

My body hurts a lot, worse than any other pain I have ever experienced. During the night, I start vomiting again. I retch violently. My stomach muscles hurt for two days. Even after there is nothing left in my stomach, I continue convulsing. I can feel I have too little water in my body. My throat is as dry as bone. I can only manage to drink a third of a cup of water, then I vomit it out again. Eventually, I take a mouthful, keep it in my mouth until it warms to body temperature, swallow a little, then a little more, and so on, until the entire mouthful is down. In this way I can keep some water down.

Saturday morning: Betsy anoints me with oil and prays for my healing again. At four o'clock in the morning the call to prayer from the mosque brings me out of my stupor. "Salat! Salat! Salat!" (come to prayer, prayer, prayer). After another half an hour, "Allahu akhbar! Allahu akhbar!" (God is the greatest). On and on it goes. I experience strong hunger pains. I drift away for a while. At five o'clock, our guard starts sweeping away the dirt outside the house. Loudly. It's the Mozambican way.

My perspiration has soaked all the way through my pillow. My pillow smells of fever. Thankfully, it is getting light outside. This always makes one feel better. Medication time again. I am still very nauseous. My kidneys hurt. I can feel them sitting there, like two warm stones. It is a very strange feeling. Arie had said that if I'm not better by ten a.m., I would have to be evacuated. Thankfully, we now have evacuation insurance, something that wasn't available for the first five years we were here.

I take the medicine. My stomach is empty. The stuff tastes terrible. My stomach contracts painfully, wanting to induce vomiting. I have another fever peak. Betsy is sponging me down, trying to keep my temperature under control. It doesn't help.

I must get under the shower again, but I do not have the strength to get there. Betsy realizes now that we have a big problem. She phones our then-core support team coordinator, Alwyn, so that he can get hold of the medical insurance company in South Africa. While she is talking to him, my stomach violently contracts again. I manage to make my way to the shower on my own. I let the water run over me. I know that when I cool down some, I don't retch so much. But then it comes again anyway. I don't want to vomit out the medication I had just taken, so I grab hold of my lips and force them to stay shut. As I vomit into my mouth, I taste the stomach acid and medicine, but then force myself to swallow it again. It works, I am able to retain the medicine.

I vomit repeatedly, keep it in and swallow it again. In the meantime, the insurance company has returned our call. The doctor asks Betsy the details regarding my temperature, medication, etc. Very professional. He approves the evacuation jet, and they go on standby some 3,000 km (2,000 miles) away. That's how remote we are. The doctor says that if any of the following happens, they will come immediately: more vomiting, delirium, no urine, or very dark urine. My urine was already quite dark, but not so bad. We decide to wait.

Around ten am. I'm starting to feel a little bit better. I feel some relief from the fever and vomiting. The saints are praying! Through the years, we have learned to "feel" the prayers of people, in the spirit. I am so grateful we don't have to wait twenty-one days like Daniel had to. We are grateful for our prayer team back in South Africa. And for God, our strength and ever present in times of trouble.

I begin to feel better, little by little. Late on Saturday afternoon Arie comes again, takes my blood pressure, and checks my liver. The medical insurance doctor calls twice a day to hear how I'm doing. We are very impressed with the response of the insurance company.

Sunday: I slept well. No more headaches! I am still very weak, but I feel okay. I know that it is going to be like this for four to five days, while my body rebuilds more red blood cells in order to get oxygen to my bodily tissue, and for the antibiotics to fight off the secondary blood infection. But praise the Lord, the worst is over.

Monday: I feel weak and tired the entire day. I can't do any work yet.

Tuesday afternoon: I feel well enough to write down this experience. Then Betsy discovers me at the computer and chases me back to bed again.

Wednesday: I am going to start working again… half-day if I can.

The Lord is always faithful. Thank you, Jesus, for sparing me so I can continue to testify of Your grace and loving kindness.

Talk the talk

Henry, Mozambique

The following story is about what we call the "three-month myth" of language learning. Most of us know someone who has told us of their cousin, friend or niece who just "picked up" a language in three months. Some language learning apps claim the same. It's a myth. However, in *this* story, it's not a myth.

Our daughter, Esté, is no ordinary girl. She's witty, clever, artistic, discerning, full of love for Jesus—and she's got a gift for languages.

Even before she could walk, she could talk, sing, and talk some more. That should have been our first clue of what was coming. Fast-forward a few years later to an outreach in Zambia, where we were showing the Jesus Film and suddenly, this twelve-year-old began talking to the Zambians, using only short phrases and words, but still talking to them. We were stunned. How did she do it? She just shrugged. Apparently, she had just "picked it up."

When we moved to Mozambique, while living in a town next to *ParkingTicket*, she mastered Portuguese in three months flat. Three months! We happily employed her as our interpreter.

How did she do it? Extrovert extraordinaire, she quickly gathered a circle of friends who spoke only Portuguese. Their common ground? Music. They were fascinated by the English songs the famous singers were singing, so she used a small dictionary and started translating lyrics for them. It turned out to be the perfect way to learn. Before long, people who didn't know her, assumed she was from Portugal. Not bad for a kid who had only just landed in Mozambique!

Later she got married and vanished over the horizon, starting her new life in America. For a time, she and her husband belonged to YWAM[12]. During their training, many of

12   Youth With a Mission

the students there were Spanish speakers. Without missing a beat, she converted her Portuguese into Spanish and was soon interpreting for them too.

Meanwhile, she was learning, well, American. She lost her South African accent so completely that Americans often ask her which state in America she is from, never guessing she wasn't born and raised in Ohio. Only her kids can detect a tiny difference between Mom's accent and Dad's. And yet, despite all these languages, she still speaks her native Afrikaans like a true "boer"—a "farmer" at heart.

One of the biggest obstacles for new missionaries is probably having to learn a new language. This story might either inspire or discourage you in your language-learning journey. Not everybody has a natural gift for languages. But with the right motivation and perseverance, you will come to a point where you can talk the talk. I promise. Even I did.

Radio funny

Betsy, Mozambique

Once a year we would take a trip to South Africa to get supplies. These trips were always exhausting. Our personal record time was four-and-a-half days. That's a four and a half days of driving twelve to fourteen hours per day, which, if you do the math, equals "way too much." It wasn't that it was so far really, only 3300 km (2062 miles), but that the roads were so terrible.

For the kids it was especially brutal. Imagine being a kid confined to a car seat for so much time, while an endless landscape of bushes and trees swept past your car window for hours. And your nightly motel is a small little tent pitched somewhere between "kind of safe" and "hope the lions don't see us."

But Esté made those trips fun. She has the gift of the gab—which is a polite way of saying, she excelled at talking. And she was *funny*. She became our in-car entertainment system. Adriaan appointed himself as the one in charge of changing the radio stations.

He'd poke her on the arm, and click, suddenly she was a weather forecaster: "And now for today's forecast: HOT, again." Another poke—click—channel changing noise—a new station: music. She'd burst into song, usually mid-chorus, just like when you tune in halfway into an actual radio station. Click—breaking news. Click—life advice for dog owners (we didn't even own a dog).

And she never ran out of material. We didn't have an entertainment system in the car, but we had her. Creative, hilarious, ingenious.

Four-and-a-half endless days of potholes, non-existing bridges over rivers, mosquitoes, and bathroom breaks in the bushes next to the road, all became tolerable because Esté had become the world's first 24-hour, ad-free, fully interactive radio station. Thanks, Esté.

Never condescend...

Henry, Mozambique

Living with the Iso was... well, let's just say "interesting." But also life-changing, rewarding, and very, very different. By this time, we were speaking Isoni fairly fluently. But drastic changes in diet, lifestyle, and stress came with their own consequences: high blood pressure and high cholesterol. I now had to take medication regularly.

Up until then, we had fasted with the Iso during Ramadan. Not because we had become Muslims, nor that we felt we *had* to fast, but because we wanted to build relationships. Here, *everyone* was fasting. This opened doors for some amazing spiritual conversations. However, this time I just couldn't. I had tried taking my medication while fasting but ended up feeling nauseous. I had to stop fasting.

One Ramadan afternoon we were visiting friends when they asked the inevitable question: "Are you fasting?" I wanted to explain the reason I couldn't fast. But how do you explain high blood pressure and cholesterol to people who have had only one or two years of schooling? I decided to get creative.

"Well," I began confidently, "inside our bodies are veins, like little pipes, that run all over inside the body. Blood flows through these pipes, but sometimes this sticky stuff forms and it gets stuck at the bends. Then the blood can't flow properly. That makes you sick. That's what happened to me. Now I need to take medicine to get rid of the sticky stuff. But if I take it on an empty stomach, I get sick. That's why we can't fast this Ramadan."

I sat back, rather pleased with my simple-yet-genius explanation. One of the women looked at me and said, "Oh, so you have a cardiovascular problem."

I nearly fell off my chair. Cardiovascular problem?! Here I was, talking about clogged up "pipes," and she was diagnosing me with the precise medical term. I instantly repented of my unintentional arrogance. They weren't the uneducated ones in that conversation. I was.

Lesson learned: Never be condescending toward uneducated people. They may be smarter than you. They just didn't have an opportunity to get educated.

The Muslim missionary

Henry, Mozambique

One day I was walking home from somewhere in the village. I saw a commotion ahead—a crowd of people gathering. Something was happening. Some excitement in the village. Like any good Iso, I pushed into the crowd to see what was going on. In the center I saw two people. The first was a big, strong Arab man dressed in a very Islamic way. He wore a long white tunic reaching his ankles and he was wearing a Muslim cap on his head. He had Muslim prayer beads in one hand while holding a huge Quran in the other. Next to him was his Mozambican clone, clothed identically in all respects, down to the prayer beads and huge Quran. He was a stranger too. Identical, except for the fact that the Mozambican man was small and scrawny.

I immediately knew this Arab man was a Muslim missionary with his interpreter. The stern and intimidating looking Arab was preaching forcefully in Arabic, and his clone was interpreting into Portuguese. They had obviously come to encourage, and probably entice, the Iso into a more radical faith. This was an unusual sight, hence the crowd of curious onlookers. What they did not seem to realize was that few Iso understood Portuguese. They may as well have been speaking French.

After a while, I saw the Arab glancing at me as he preached. "Why look at me?," you might ask. Well, one possibility could be that I was the only light-skinned person in the crowd. I could see that he was becoming nervous. He had noticed that, while he was obviously a novelty there, nobody was looking at me, even though I stood out like a sore thumb. I could sense the questions going through his mind: "What is this white man doing here?" "Why is nobody even noticing him?" "What does he know that I don't?" This was rather funny. *I* was supposed to be the outsider, not him, a fellow Muslim.

After a while, I almost started feeling sorry for him. Chuckling inwardly, I left. His knowledge of missiology[13] was sorely lacking. I remembered that this was the reason we had decided to learn Isoni—to be able to communicate with the Iso in their mother tongue, and to become a part of the community. We did all of this with the objective of being able to share the gospel with them effectively in their own language and in the context of their culture. The Arab and his Portuguese interpreter would always be outsiders and foreigners. And now, I had become an Iso.

"... I have become all things to all people so that by all possible means I might save some" (1 Corinthians 9:20-34).

Road ratings in Africa—a humoristic analysis

Henry, Mozambique

A recent trip led me to do some deep thinking concerning the rating of road conditions in Africa. This formal dissertation is the result of said introspection.

---

13   The study of cross-cultural missions.

My experience when asking people about road conditions in Mozambique, and other African countries, has been one of frustration. Some people, whom I shall call the "Macho Brigade," always say, "Easy going, no problem." Their macho "no problem" roads might be characterized by washed-away bridges or ferries that are not running. Not to mention bone-crunching, head-hitting, teeth-grinding, "slightly bumpy" roads. Or the macho missionary might say, "It was slow going," which to the rest of us means slipping, sliding and slithering through knee-deep mud and muck, the car sometimes facing forty-five degrees away from the direction in which you are steering. "Macho Brigaders" also neglect to mention the near coronary conditions that exist when one hears the foghorn warning of a monster truck, slithering and sliding across the road, bearing right down on you. The monster truck driver urges you to get out of the way, because *he* can't control *his* vehicle—as if *you* can!

People at the other end of the scale, among whom I classify myself, are referred to as the "Wimp Brigade." They rate any road short of the most smooth, wide, well-marked highway as "nightmarish."

To make things more complicated, each individual driver is at a different point on the scale between "Macho Brigade" and "Wimp Brigade." Now the difficulty is this: How do you determine the macho level of the person telling you the road conditions? How do you map the road conditions according to *his* point of view to *your* point of view?

As academics would say: Field research needs to be done by practitioners to quantify and classify road conditions into understandable levels. This is done by analyzing the empirical data and mapping the data into a suitable theoretical framework. This can lead to productive theorizing in order to build a basis for future research.

Don't worry. I don't know what that means either.

But how does one start objectively rating the roads? Maybe it's good enough to say that the very best roads in Mozambique are slightly worse than the worst roads in, say, Europe. All except the toll road to the capital of Maputo, of course. But give it time. Time is the great equalizer in Africa. Or maybe one could start by saying a road is a hundred percent better than driving through an area where no other car has ever gone before. Yes, that sounds like a positive approach. Or maybe one could work on a scale of one to ten, where one is the best highway in Europe, and ten is a virgin piece of swampland where no vehicle has ever been before.

But even that would not yet tell the whole story. Which is worse? A dirt road that has never been paved over with asphalt, or one where only small tire-ripping pieces of tar surfacing remain? When is a tarred road potholed, and when is it actually really a dirt road with tar islands? Which should be rated worse—getting stuck in stinky, swamp mud, or on sea-sand with the tide coming in?

When people ask me on what side of the road we drive on Mozambique, I would answer, "In South Africa we drive on the *left* side of the road. In Germany they drive on the *right* side of the road. In Mozambique we drive on the *best* side of the road." The best side varies from place to place. On a good, surfaced road, it would be in the middle of the road. This way you avoid vendors that suddenly rush out from behind a bush with an upside-down squawking chicken in hand, wanting to make a sale. Or a squawking chicken running across the road on its own. Or a wayward goat.

Elsewhere, left side is best, especially with oncoming traffic, or if traffic officers are nearby. On badly potholed roads, it would be off-the-left-side or off-the-right-side depending on many factors, such as: whether there is a deep ditch or not, whether there are pedestrians, or oncoming monster trucks with booming foghorns. Then there is what I call the "sine-wave side," which means weaving between both-sides-and-in-the-middle, depending on where the potholes are.

How then does one rate these roads? With all of the above in mind, I have come up with the Vermont **R**oad-**Q**uality **S**cale or *VRQS*.

The first section of the VRQS is the RTR: **R**oad **T**ype **R**ating. RTR-**T** is for **T**ar surfaced roads. RTR-**D** is for **D**irt roads. Then we have the RTR-**TD**, which is used for **T**ar roads that have become **D**irt roads through time and use. This should not be confused with RTR-**DT**, which is **D**irt roads where **T**ar roads are being built.

Dry Dirt Roads can be rated according to the top speed achievable without resulting in the total destruction of your vehicle. And note that the vehicle is assumed to be a tough four-wheel drive, not a Toyota Corolla.

- 80km/h+: RTR-DE (**E**xcellent)
- 60km/h+: RTR-DG (**G**ood)
- 45km/h+: RTR-DM (**M**edium)
- 20km/h+: RTR-DB (**B**ad)
- 10km/h+: RTR-DT (**T**errible)
- Slower: RTR-DA (**A**trocious)

"Terrible" (RTR-DT) is easily recognizable by the low speed on the speedometer (if you dare take your eyes off the road), the fighting against the steering wheel which takes on a life of its own, and the banging of the passengers' heads against the car windows. "Atrocious" is like "Terrible," except that the driver's head also bangs against the window.

"Bad" is often accompanied by the occasional "donk" sound as passengers' heads hit the ceiling. This on its own doesn't qualify as a downgrading to "Terrible."

Tar Surfaced Roads can be rated as follows. The indicated speeds should be seen as an absolute maximum possible:

- RTR-TE (**E**xcellent) 120km/h+ (75mph) is possible, without a possibility of hitting people, goats or chickens. Most European highways for the most part would be a good example of this.

- RTR-TG (**G**ood) 120km/h+ (75mph) is possible, with a higher-than-normal probability of hitting people, goats or chickens. If you kill an animal in Mozambique, you have to pay the owner the monetary value of the now-deceased animal. Always remember that goats are more expensive than chickens.

- RTR-TM (**M**edium) 100km/h+ (62mph); same as "**G**ood," but with potholes with a radius of no more than 30cm (1 ft) and spaced no less than 100m (±100 yards) apart. There is a distinct possibility of hitting potholes, people, goats or chickens. When traveling such roads, be sure to know the going price of goats and chickens before departure.

- RTR-TB (**B**ad) 100km/h+ (62mph); same as "**M**edium," except that pothole sizes have increased and spacing has decreased. Please note that the biggest potholes have been positioned just after blind rises, especially designed so as not to be seen. Due to your increased alertness to potholes, the chances of hitting people, goats or chickens have increased. The chance of bending an axle has exponentially increased as well.

- RTR-TT (**T**errible) 60km/h (37mph) or less. The percentage of potholes versus tar now tends toward 50-50. Keep to the "sine wave" (usable) side of the road, or even better, the off-to-the-left side or the off-to-the-right side. Hitting people has become unlikely, unless you concentrate solely on the potholes. But keep in mind that even goats sometimes like to play "chicken."
- RTR-TA (**A**trocious) Speed approaches zero. People and animals are quite safe. Even tortoises.

An extra "S" in brackets may be added to the above codes like this [S]. This stands for "with **S**urprises." An example of this would be when you are driving on a perfectly well surfaced tar road when suddenly a temporary bridge appears before you, with a ramp so steep that it causes you to momentarily lose traction on all four wheels—because all four are airborne at the same time. Or, of course, it could be the unexpected car-sized, one-story deep pothole that is waiting for you just over the blind rise. [MS] means "Many Surprises." [S] and [MS] may only be used to refer to RTR-TE, RTR-TG and RTR-TM. The worst ones are automatically full of surprises the entire time.

What are the practical implications of this road rating system? How could it be used to improve the lives of missionaries? I can easily visualize two Macho Brigaders, fully equipped with Camel-Trophy labeled khaki clothes, boots, and Leathermans[14] on their belts discussing a recent trip in the local off-road shop.

Using the VRQS-system, they could easily express themselves fully and understandably. Even other shoppers, pretending to browse through high-lift jacks and designer shovels, would be able to eavesdrop and be impressed by their efficient description of road conditions:

"Yeah, once we passed Maputo, the RTR-TE suddenly became RTR-TG. After Xai-Xai it degraded further to RTR-TM with some sections of RTR-TM[S]. But man, the best part was the road from Dondo to Caia, which was RTR-DM most of the way, but with many great strips of true RTR-DA. Some of the less-experienced people in our convoy got stuck, but nothing *I* couldn't solve with my winch and high-lift jack." Does that sound sufficiently macho? Impressive? Surely!

Where does this take us? What does the future hold for VRQS? I can see further empirical research being done into, for example, mud ratings. This would have to include depth and slipperiness factors, possibly the smell of swampy areas, and the likelihood of which times of the year mud could be expected. These ratings should bring a boom to the off-road driver training centers. Who knows? Maybe the Civil Engineering Departments of one of the universities could offer road-rating studies at post-graduate level. The academic possibilities are boundless.

---

14 A multi-tool that typically includes pliers and various other tools like knives, screwdrivers, and can openers, all in a compact design.

"You must be very stupid"

Henry, Mozambique

Life was good. We could now communicate quite well in Isoni. We were feeling rather clever, if I may say so. We almost had it all figured out.

One afternoon, we visited a family whose matriarch had officially adopted us as her children. Along with the privilege of her being our *Mama,* came all kinds of unexpected responsibilities. She didn't ask, she insisted. Strangely, we didn't complain about it—it made us feel like we belonged.

And so there we were, happily sitting together, when *Mama* suddenly started staring at me. I tried to ignore it, but after a while I had to say something.

"What are you looking at?" I asked.

She replied calmly, "I'm thinking."

"Thinking about what?" I asked, trying to sound patient.

"I'm just thinking … you must be *really* stupid."

Excuse me? Stupid? Me? I could feel the pride rising inside me. Really? I had an education. I could speak four languages. She had barely finished two years of school. *Stupid? Really?*

I held my pose, took a deep breath, and asked as graciously as I could, "Why do you say that?"

She pointed at a two-year-old playing in the dirt. "That little girl was born after you came here, and she speaks Isoni better than you." I was speechless. That was true. She was right. I *must* be pretty stupid.

When pride comes, disgrace follows, but with humility comes wisdom (Proverbs 11:2).

The parable of the rich new neighbor

Henry

Why do missionaries need to learn the language and the culture of the people they are living with? Come with me on an imaginary journey to see it from the other side...

You're living in suburban bliss in a well-off Western country. On Saturday afternoons, you're lulled to sleep by the gentle hum of lawnmowers and the smell of barbecue in the air. Kids are riding their bicycles up and down the street, laughing and playing. The reassuring *chi-chi-chi* sound lets you know your irrigation sprayers are watering the lawn. Now and then, a car cruises by slowly with families looking for a house to buy, or maybe they're just on a Saturday afternoon drive. You have a warm, fuzzy feeling in your heart at the familiarity and security of it all.

And then, one day, it all changes for the worse. New neighbors have moved into the big house to your left. They are very strange looking indeed. *Very.* They have strange hair, strange clothes, strange everything. It is soon obvious that they are also filthy rich. They own a fancy car *and* a boat.

Fortunately, they are very friendly. The husband comes over to say hello every day. He can scarcely speak English, so he's employed a full-time interpreter through whom he speaks to you.

Unfortunately, he seems very dirty to you. It's not that he stinks—he rubs some kind of paste on his skin which gives off an odor when comes over to greet you. When you ask him about it, he just laughs and says that's just the way they do it back home—it protects them from the sun.

You suppose that's okay, but what's concerning to you is the fact that when you see his wife in their front yard, she's topless. You are so scandalized, you don't know where to look. What will your kids learn think? They will *not* miss a thing like that. Apparently, that is normal for them, that's how they dress back home.

They also belong to some weird religious sect that you find offensive. When they pray, they offer birds as sacrifice to their god. The men and women pray together naked. He's very vocal about his religion, too. His cars are covered with slogans about his religion and his gods in your language, even though you know very well he can't even speak it well.

Then the day comes when he tries to convert you to his religion. Because he doesn't understand your culture and the routines of your life, he and his interpreter arrive just at the time for your evening meal. Yet you remain polite because you don't want to offend. You remain polite as he explains his weird religion to you. You can't relate to it; it even offends you. Moreover, it turns out that, if you would choose to follow his religion, you will also have to wear the weird clothes he wears, sacrifice birds and so on. What would they say at work? You'd probably get fired! And, of course, he goes on and on about how your religion is false, his is the only true religion.

Would you ever consider changing to his religion, even if he could convince you of its truth?

A ridiculous story. But is it really so ridiculous? Indulge me some more and let's look at how this story corresponds with reality in other parts of the world...

Imagine yourself as the average Muslim. You are poor. Few people you know even own bicycles. You know you have the true, pure religion. One out of every six people on the planet follows your religion, and it is the fastest growing religion in the world. So it must be the best one. For a thousand years, your ancestors have known these truths. Islam permeates your society, affecting culture, politics, business, and your whole way of life is intertwined with your belief system.

You've heard at mosque of Christians and their blasphemies—praying to three gods while everyone *knows* that God is one god. You've peered into their churches and seen the detestable idols they worship. And, worst of all, you've heard that they say that the great prophet Jesus was the Son of God—yet you know God would never have intercourse with a woman. Such blasphemy! You've read the Quran that says that Jesus was killed on a cross by men. Yet you know that God would never allow such a thing to happen to one of His holy prophets!

You have seen some of the scandalous Christian movies on your friend's television. They even show men and women sleeping together. Because your religion is such an integral part of your society, you assume that their religion must be integral to their lives too. So these must be Christian movies because they come from America, a Christian country. No wonder everyone calls it the "Great Satan."

One day a stranger arrives in his car. He owns that car, so he must be filthy rich. He moves into the large house to your left. He calls himself a "missionary," which means he is here to tear you away from your society and your values. He is unclean—you know his whole family eats pork. You don't want to touch him or let him drink out of your teacups, because then you would be unclean too, and you would not be able to pray. But, on the positive side, at least he is very friendly and helpful. Therefore you tolerate him. You don't see any idols, but you know he's got them hidden somewhere.

The interpreter he has employed is one of your own people. A traitor who's left the ways of his forefathers to follow the false religion of Christianity.

All the neighbors are talking about his wife who is scandalizing the community by walking around without a head covering. The shame of it!

His car is covered with offensive slogans such as "Jesus is Lord" and "Christ." And to make things worse, his wife is actually wearing a cross as a pendant around her neck. You've seen him reading his holy book in his garden while he's patting his dog. And everyone knows that if a dog, an unclean creature, even sniffs at you that you are ritually unclean and can't pray—and touching a holy book while doing so is pure blasphemy! A friend tells you that he once glanced into their church and saw with his own eyes how the men and women sit together there, and could you believe it, the women were without head coverings, as good as being naked. He said that everyone was wearing shoes. In a holy place? How can God withhold His judgment from them?

Then the day comes when he tries to convert you to his religion. He and his interpreter arrive at a very inopportune time, just as you are about to leave for the mosque. Yet you remain polite. You remain so as he explains his weird religion —you can't relate to it; it even offends you. If you follow his religion, you assume that you will also have to wear the weird Western clothes he does, start eating pork, touching dogs, worshiping with semi-naked women, and so on. Your family would kick you out, for sure. Then you'd have no income because you can't work for the family business anymore. And yet he goes on and on about how your religion is all false, that *his* is the only true religion. How offensive and presumptuous.

> *"And to the Jews I became as a Jew, so that I might gain the Jews. To those who are under the Law, I became as under the Law, so that I might gain those who are under the Law. To those who are outside Law, I became as outside Law (not being outside law to God, but under the law to Christ), so that I might gain those who are outside Law. To the weak I became as the weak, so that I might gain the weak. I am made all things to all men, so that I might by all means save some. And this I do for the sake of the gospel, so that I might be partaker of it with you"* (1 Corinthians 9:20-23).

The demon who understood Isoni

Henry, Mozambique

The text from Betsy was short and urgent: "Come right now!" My heart skipped a beat, and I walked as fast as I could to the house where I knew she'd be. Something must be terribly wrong—she had never sent me a message like that before.

When I reached the yard of our Iso friends, I immediately understood the urgency. A woman from a neighboring country was visiting them. She spoke a language related to Isoni, so they understood each other. Betsy and her friends had been baking bread, when this young woman suddenly went rigid—as stiff as a board. She became completely still, her back went taut, and her unfocused eyes just stared into the air. Betsy sensed immediately what was happening. But she just asked her friends as casually and

114

calmly as possible, "What's wrong with her?" "Oh, she has a *Genie,*" they replied casually while carrying on kneading dough.

A *Genie.* Not a funny blue one that grants wishes like in the Aladdin movie. No, this was no cartoon character, and it certainly wasn't funny. Muslims around the world believe in *jinn* (or *jini* or *genies)* who are said to be part human, part demon. To them this isn't fantasy. It's a reality embedded in the deepest part of their culture, their worldview. Even in countries like Saudi Arabia, with their "pure" Islam, such beliefs are part of everyday life.

By the time I arrived, the woman was no longer stiff. Instead, she was now hopping around the yard, like a rabbit gone mad. Even though her eyes were shut tightly, she would hop over to people and shake their hands. Then she stopped and gripped her own head in both hands and began violently twisting it. It was clear that something inside her wanted to kill her.

Suddenly she began running as fast as she could and slammed her head against a cement cistern so hard that the force rattled the heavy structure. She threw herself against it over and over again, and yet, shockingly, no marks appeared on her head.

Everybody there, watching her, were Muslims. I was torn about how to respond to this crisis, probably out of both caution and fear. At first, I commanded the demon to leave, in Afrikaans. Nothing happened. She just ran and bashed her head against the cistern again. I rebuked the demon again, this time in Portuguese. Still nothing. Finally, I mustered my best Isoni and commanded the demon to leave, in the name of Jesus.

And instantly—as if a switch had been flipped—she came fully to her senses. She stopped, stood still, looking around her in confusion. Then, embarrassed, she ran into the house. Our Iso friends were astonished. "What is all this 'In the name of Jesus'?," they asked. It was already dark by then so we told them we would return the next morning to explain.

There is power in the name of Jesus. We can testify to this reality, no matter how strange this story may seem to you.

By the next morning, the woman was gone. She had left in the night and had gone back, across the border to her own country. We had no way to follow up with her. And the biggest disappointment to us was that, even after such a dramatic incident, the family were suddenly not interested in learning more about Jesus.

But God reminded us of Jesus who healed the Gerasene demoniac—it seemed that only he had an appreciation and understanding of Jesus' authority, because Matthew 8:34 tells us, *after this spectacular deliverance, the whole town went out to meet Jesus. And when they saw Him, they begged Him to leave their region.*

A friend who is closer than a brother

Betsy, Mozambique

The sun was just setting. The sky was filled with deep orange and red hues, with a tint of purple. The waves were softly lapping. The sand on the beach had finally started to cool down, and it felt good to wriggle our toes in it. A tub of ice cream, finger cookies, and a group of friends hanging out on the beach, just enjoying the coolness of the day.

It was Henry and me, our two kids and Lizette, a fellow South African. She was in her early thirties. She was the project manager of an orphanage in the nearby town, had overseen its construction, organized everything, appointed staff, and set the whole operation in motion—an impressive feat, to say the least. Enthusiastic, joyful, dynamic, a Jesus-lover, and our best friend.

We lived with the Iso in *ParkingTicket*, and she lived on the grounds of the orphanage in town. It was two different worlds. And yet, she always knew just when to show up. Unexpectedly, she would arrive at our house in the village and, with a loud voice, "demand" coffee. The whole house would suddenly explode with energy and fun.

The coffee—well, it was powdered, instant coffee with powdered milk, but for us, it was the fanciest latte around! The kids called it "Whipped Coffee" (*klitskoffie*). In Afrikaans it sounded like a fancy choice from a coffee shop. The kids would first add a little cold water to the coffee, milk powder and a lot of sugar and whip it aggressively until it looked somewhat foamy. Then they added the boiled water. There it was—"Whipped Coffee à la Moz."

Sometimes Lizette would invite us over to her place to watch a movie on her TV—the whole lot of us, plus her little dog Rocky, squashed onto her bed. And then she would bring out the snacks. I never knew where she got them from. Living in the orphanage compound, she usually got electricity from a generator. For a short while we could escape from our hot, steamy, stinky house on the toilet beach in the Iso village to this haven of modernity.

And then, sometimes, she pulled her "magic trick." Out of the blue she would ask us to meet her on the beach or somewhere else. That beach was a clean one, about ten miles away. Knowing her, we would just drop everything and go immediately! And soon we would all be sitting together on the beach, giggling and eating ice cream with finger cookies, watching the sunset.

Sounds all too perfect, right? Well, let me be honest. The ice cream she got from a little store in town had gone through a few cycles of defrosting, melting, and freezing again. The finger cookies were old and hard—but that made them perfect spoons.

We didn't care. We were a "band of brothers and sisters." We shared memories, hardships and good times that nobody else would understand. This stretch of beach is also where Henry baptized her and our son Adriaan together, and later the first Iso believers—this was a very special place for us.

God used her, and is still using her, just at the right moments, to remind us of a God who cares, a God who, in His lovingkindness, puts people like Lizette in our lives to lift us up when we are down, to laugh with us when we celebrate, and to walk beside us as like-minded nomads. Thanks, Lizette.

… there is a friend who stays closer than a brother (Proverbs 18:24).

CHAPTER SIX

BIBLE STORIES THAT TRANSFORM

―――――⬥⬥⬥―――――

One story at a time

Henry, Mozambique

From the beginning, we knew that the Iso were mostly illiterate so we would have to follow a "paperless" route of evangelism and discipleship. This was long before we knew that such a thing as "oral learners" existed, and that there were strategies to reach people who learned by listening, rather than by reading the written word.

When we first arrived in Isoland, I had met up with a missionary who was moving elsewhere. He had been there for about ten years. I sat him down, asking him about everything he and his team had done to try reaching the Iso. I was determined not to attempt the same things they had if these methods hadn't borne fruit. The list was long, as this man had worked really hard.

Listening to him I felt a bit discouraged. He and his team had tried many approaches to have a breakthrough among the Iso: Public evangelism events, public debates, one-on-one evangelism, teaching people to read, using local believers from a nearby people group to do door-to-door evangelism. On and on the list went.

But there was one thing he hadn't tried—telling Bible stories chronologically, starting with the Old Testament. Therefore, by way of elimination, we decided that this would be our approach. But this approach had many implications. The Bible was not yet available in Isoni. We would have to translate the chronological teachings and use the as-yet unpublished New Testament portions the Bible translators had already translated.

But where there's a will, there's a way. Zuba, an Iso man who was fluent in Iso and Portuguese, had been my language helper for a year and a bit. And now he would become my translation consultant. For many months I met up with him daily, translating a series of chronological Bible teachings called "Building on Firm Foundations" from Portuguese into Isoni. In the process I also adapted the stories to better fit the Iso culture.

On the way to Zuba's house, I always passed by Zuberi's house. Zuberi sold rice from his veranda, his house being next to a busy road. Most days, I would walk past him on my way to Zuba. Usually, he had four or five of his friends sitting there with him, keeping him company. Like any good Iso, he would always ask questions as I walked past: "Where are you going?," "Why are you going there?," and so on. From the beginning I always said, "To Zuba, he's helping me learn Isoni."

Once Zuba and I began our translation work, I just kept on telling Zuberi, "I'm going to Zuba." Eventually, after some time had passed, Zuberi and his friends asked, "Why are you still going to Zuba? You already speak Isoni."

Knowing I was speaking to a group of Muslims, I didn't want to cause trouble for Zuba by mentioning the word "Bible," so I said, "He's helping me translate the books of Moses." In Islam, Moses, or Musa, is one of the great prophets, after Muhammad and Jesus, of course. They seemed interested. At that moment I had a flash of inspiration. I said to them, "Did you know that the Quran says that God has revealed the *Tawrat*[15], and in it there is a guidance and light? It also says that those who do not believe in the Tawrat "are no better than unbelievers."

Like good Muslims, they all said, "Yes, we know that" but I'm not sure that they did. I asked, "Are you following that guidance and light?" Silence. I continued, "So that's what Zuba and I are doing. We're translating the stories of the books of Moses into Isoni, so that you can have that guidance and light." That got their attention.

They said, "We want to hear this. When will you be finished?" I said I would tell them when we were finished. Almost every day from then on, they asked me, "When, when?" I jokingly said to Betsy that this was my "curiosity evangelism" approach.

Months later Zuberi and his group were the first Iso men to hear these chronological Bible teachings. Later, we would record these lessons and put them on MP3 players—but you will read more about what transpired in the next chapters.

The empty nest

15 "Tawrat" is the Arabic word for the Torah, the first five books of the Bible—the books of Moses. This is a paraphrase of Surah 5:54.

Betsy, Mozambique

After Esté finished high school at home and passed her SAT tests, she went back to South Africa. There, she started her ministry with an evangelistic performing arts group called "C-Kruis" (later "13th Floor"). Adriaan became very lonely without his sister's company, and just a few months after she had left, he asked us to let him go to boarding school at the King's School in South Africa. Discovering this Christian school was yet another *God-incidence*, because it had a small boarding house with only a few students. It was more like a real home than a boarding house.

Esté excelled after leaving Mozambique, taking the reverse culture shock in her stride. After completing her year with *C-Kruis*, she was given the honor of joining *13th Floor*'s team to visit America. During that time, she met her future husband, Matt.

After a hard first six months of adapting to living back in "civilization," Adriaan started excelling in school. He became popular with his schoolmates and an overachiever academically. We always knew he was clever, but not to the extent he turned out to be.

So suddenly, within a period of just four short months, we were empty nesters. We missed the kids terribly, so we filled every empty hour we had with ministry—which had grave repercussions later on.

Tips and hacks for nomads

Betsy, Mozambique

Nomads live in deserts, ride camels or horses and do not have a fixed address. They know where to find water and can navigate over vast areas of sand dunes and barren land. But I'm not talking about those kinds of nomads.

I'm talking about cultural nomads—a cool name for missionaries.

> *Hear my prayer O Lord and give ear to my cry. Do not be silent at my tears, for I am a stranger with you, a sojourner like all my fathers* (Psalm 39:12).

Like nomads, missionaries often do not have a fixed abode. They ride in off-road vehicles or use crazy public transport and sometimes live in scary places. They must navigate their way through a maze of different customs, learn how to sleep anywhere and become comfortable with loneliness and isolation. In our case, we learned to endure three-day-long wedding ceremonies in extreme heat, all the while being packed in a small space with hundreds of people. Personal space? Not here. It doesn't exist.

Cultural nomads are often confronted with problems they never even knew existed. They need to learn to really trust God, be flexible, *and* to have a sense of humor. Without those they are in big trouble. Especially the sense of humor.

In Afrikaans we say "'n Boer maak 'n plan" which literally means, "A farmer makes a plan." That is, if something goes wrong on a farm, they must find a way around it, figure it out. The same goes for missionaries too. Like they say, "You gotta do what you gotta do!"

One of the first things we had to do upon arriving in Mozambique, was to go through the bureaucratic complications of importing our car, something totally new to us. This all had to be done in Portuguese, a language we were just learning. We used a dictionary in the presence of impatient and inflexible officials, thankfully we had that prerequisite sense of humor. We smiled a lot, prayed a lot, and trusted God for the impossible. Eventually we got our car's registration papers.

But there was one small hiccup, however. There was no shop there that could make the car's registration plates. Yes, really. After a desperate search, with the dictionary in hand, we found a man with a workshop in the middle of a mud-hut village. He was able to cut two steel plates of the right size for us. They weighed a ton.

Then we found another man who could paint them, a black background with white letters painted on it. By hand. It looked very hand-made, which it was. Done. Right? No!

Thankfully we picked up a mistake the official had made —he had given us the wrong registration number! We discovered this just as the senior official was on his way to complete the final inspection. We knew that *we* would have to pay the fine for this inexcusable error—that's how it works there. We had to make a plan, and quickly!

All I had was some typist's correction fluid in a small bottle with an even smaller brush. Hurriedly, I modified those number plates. They were done just in time. We passed the inspection. The very same number plate with its artsy, hand-painted number stayed true and clear until we sold the car ten years later. It had survived, even after regularly passing through sea sand, water and mud.

Here's another nomad tip: The name "Mozambique" means "Mosquito-land." Just kidding. But this country was notorious for being malaria-infested. We used to joke, saying, "There isn't a *single* mosquito in Mozambique. They are all married and have thousands of little mozzy kids."

We always brought stacks of supplies of antibiotic creams and ointments from South Africa to relieve itching mosquito and other insect bites. But we invariably ran out of supplies within a few months. The biting was relentless. So was the itching. What could we do? Someone once told us to rub toothpaste onto the bites. We tried it and what a relief. Yes, it really worked. And we smelled nice and minty. And, you could use your tooth-pasted arm hairs to get a good floss too. Nah, not really!

This toothpaste tradition carried on even when we moved to Southeast Asia years later, even though we could buy anti-itch cream at any pharmacy there. The toothpaste treatment was far superior. And cheaper.

We had a book with us called *"Where there is no doctor."* We used it a lot—because during the first few years we lived in Mozambique the closest qualified doctor was many hours of driving away, and the closest qualified dentist was in the neighboring country, about two days' drive away. There was no way we could drive that far in an emergency.

We sure used that book often. We soon saw a pattern in the book—simple, easy to remember, yet effective. You have malaria? Drink water. You cut your toe? Drink water. You are feeling sorry for yourself? Drink water. Get the idea? If you don't, drink some water.

Henry's back had a bad habit of "popping out." It's painful. What do you do with no doctors, no dentists, and certainly no chiropractors nearby? A missionary colleague once showed me how to manipulate it so the vertebrae would click back into place. And that's how I became Henry's official "back-fixer." To this day, I'm his first line of treatment. If I fail to fix it, then he'll go to a real chiropractor. I've saved us a small fortune. He never pays me, though. Stingy man.

You'll read later on what I can do with super glue. A hint —it has something to do with dentistry in the bush.

Anything broken or rattling? Cable ties, steel epoxy putty, and binding wire became our go-to solutions. Of course these items didn't work for our minds or emotions, only for physical things.

During our first year in Mozambique, we only had a radio for communication. No phones. Nothing. This was no radio to play music or to listen to the news. It was an amateur "ham" radio. Remember, Henry was (still is) a bit of a nerd. He never thought that the amateur radio license he got many years before would come in handy in ministry one day.

At weddings and other ceremonies, it was expected of us to eat with our Iso friends. This would involve about eight people sitting cross-legged on a mat around a big tin plate with a huge mound of rice on it, with either some bits of goat stew or beans on top of it. Everyone ate with their hands, so we had to do the same. Now, for Muslims the left hand is unclean, because—how to put this delicately, that hand has... bathroom duties... I'll say no more.

That means we had to learn to eat using only our right hand. The problem is that when we scooped some rice with our right hand, some always fell off. Your automatic reaction is to catch the rice with your left hand. *Haraam*[16]!

We managed to come up with a brilliant life hack to stop ourselves from using the left hand instinctively, thereby not having to run the risk of offending our friends. We started sitting on our left hands. Problem solved. No accidental left-hand catching falling rice. Genius, if you ask me.

Here's another hack: When water was scarce, we were able to wash with one liter (two pints) of water. This includes washing your hair and the whole body. This hack was tested once when a prayer team came to visit, right in the middle of a "no water" period. We had saved up some water in a tank on the roof, but we didn't know when the water supply would be resumed again. We needed to be stingy with our water. We trained the team on the "one-liter method." How precious it was when we found one of them, standing in the dry shower, fully dressed, praying for water.

The hack I'm most proud of was being able to cut my own hair. I had no choice, if I wanted to look halfway decent. There were no hairdressers nearby. We only went to South Africa once a year, remember. I even mastered the art of trimming the hair at the back of my head without accidentally giving myself a lobotomy. Word spread. A missionary friend heard about my "amazing skills with hair" and asked me to cut her hair too. I was very nervous. And then it happened… I clipped her ear by mistake—there was blood *everywhere.* It was an accident. Really! I thought, "Well, that settles it. She'll never ask me again." To my horror… she did. Apparently, a free haircut is worth shedding a little blood for.

16 Arabic word meaning forbidden or unclean.

While hacking our way through different countries and sometimes extreme situations, the incidents were either funny or critical. Looking back now I have a sense of awe, knowing that God went before us, with us, carrying us, and yes, laughing with us, too. He has a sense of humor, for sure.

*...for the joy of the LORD is your strength (*Nehemiah 8:10).

Stolen for a purpose

Henry, Mozambique

Background to this story: In Isoni, the first five books of the Bible are called the *Taureti*, from the Hebrew *Torah* or Arabic *Tawrat*. Muslims accept the *Torah* as part of their scriptures, but very few have actually read it. And hidden inside those pages are some very significant truths that point straight to Christ. Here is what happened with the first batch of *Tauretis*.

One day, it seemed that disaster had struck. A missionary from a village to the north of us was transporting a batch of Tauretis in the back of his car. That was, until the car got broken into. A whole batch of invaluable Isoni Tauretis was stolen. Gone. Poof. These were about a quarter of all the Tauretis ever printed, and there was no printing press within 3200 km (2000 miles) where we could reprint them, and no budget to do it with anyway. Can you imagine the disappointment we all felt. Losing that many Scripture portions was a big blow to all of us—or so it seemed—until God stepped in.

A few months later, this same missionary was driving through the middle of nowhere when he stopped to give a lift to an Iso man. They chatted for a while, and then the man casually started talking about Moses, Noah, and other Old Testament prophets.

Curious, the missionary asked him how he knew all this. The man said, "Oh, I read it in a book. It's called the Taureti." Stunned, the missionary asked the man where he had found such a book. The man replied, "I bought it from a stall in a little village nearby."

And just like that, what once seemed to be a great tragedy turned out to be… God's distribution plan, which was, of course, much more effective than anything any of us could have come up with.

This is more proof that the Lord can use any situation—even a heist—for the good of His Kingdom.

And we know that God works all things together for the good of those who love Him, who are called according to His purpose (Romans 8:28).

Beauty and the beast

Betsy, Mozambique

You know the saying, "If all else fails, smile." Well, there was one time when it was awfully difficult for me to smile.

The Iso women loved to do their hair in a certain way. They liked to pull sections of their hair and twist them into very tight balls, resulting in many little balls of hair all over their heads.

They desperately wanted me to look more Iso, and they tried many times to "fix" my hair. At long last, the kids managed to get my hair to look just right. I was amazed that my hair could stay put in those tight little balls all over my head. As I was walking home soon after, shouts of admiration and good-natured laughter followed me. Everyone just loved my new hairstyle. One granny even clapped her hands and shouted, "Now you are a real Iso!" Here is the first reason I could not smile that day—my hair was pulled back so tightly, that I could barely speak, never mind smile. It felt as if my skin was also pulled back into one big ball. This was a free alternative to having a face lift.

I finally arrived home, quite pleased with my new Iso-look, and the positive reaction I had received from the Iso. And now, the second reason for not smiling that day: Henry gave me one startled look, and said, "Just stand there. Don't move! I need to find the camera to take a photo of you. This is the *ugliest* you have ever looked."

Words—and smiles—failed me. Henry thought it was hilarious! Me? Not so much. I never tried that style again.

A tale of two Toyotas

An *auto* biography

Toyota Hilux Raider, Africa

Hi. You probably don't know me. My name is Raider. Raider AHT33GNG508000062, to be exact. My last name is Toyota. No, I'm not an alien. I'm a car. I'm from the Toyota clan. My heritage may be Japanese, but I was born in South Africa. Just another one from a long line of Toyota brothers, all faithful and true. From birth, I thought that my most challenging task would be climbing pavements whenever my owner could not find parking. Boy, was I ever wrong. My life turned out to be anything but boring...

Many a time I have told my tale to other cars parked next to me. Usually, my stories were met by incredulous disbelief radiating from their…umm…radiators. Well, I have now decided to tell my story to the world.

I started out as quite the star. Literally. Within the first 500 km (310 miles) I drove, I was featured in a photo shoot as the firstborn of a new line of models. Yes, that's the truth. I thought that, despite my newfound fame, I would eventually be relegated to do the boring back-and-forth driving from a showroom to a salesman's home, and back to the showroom again. This was not meant to be.

One day I overheard the salesman speaking to my owner-to-be. He was a missionary going to Mozambique. I was being sold into slavery in Mozambique! I had heard the tales of unbearable hardships from my older cousins. Tales of aching shock absorbers, sneezing from the dust in their air filters, being buried in mud, and sometimes even having to remain idle for hours on end, waiting for ferries to cross the rivers. The horror of it.

Then one day, there he was. My new owner. He looked like a bit of an idiot but he seemed nice enough—if you like beards on humans. But man, did that man's big butt put pressure on my front seat. Still, he looked like someone who'd look after me, take care of me. I prefer to think of him and his wife as Mum and Dad. He was a bit of a joker, too. Parents can be *so* embarrassing.

I soon came to realize that my days of hanging around with beautiful actresses posing on my hood, under bright lights in front of snapping cameras, had come to an abrupt end. I realized this when Dad took me to Zambia on an outreach trip. On the way there I had to swerve sharply to miss some elephants who were casually strolling along in the middle of the road. I had to splash through pools of mud, bounce through potholes, wade through a river. The muddy water rushing over my hood sure ruined my good looks.

Next came major surgery. Dad took me to some tough-looking characters who enlarged my stomach so that I could hold more gas, so I could go further without getting thirsty too soon. What am I, a camel? It turned out that I needed it though. Then I got a hat, or shall I say a canopy covering my load bed. I knew that this was bad news—they were going to make me carry a *lot* of stuff in there. And was I right. But little did I suspect that this would be the least of my worries.

They had decided to get me a partner. What an unequal partnership this turned out to be. I got a trailer friend. A trailer with lots of drawers to carry supplies. Sure, *Trailey* (as I like to call him) had to carry a lot of stuff, but *I* had to do the pulling. Man, my back still aches when I think back. Dad called *Trailey* his "chest of drawers on wheels." I still remember my new *Trailey* brother fondly whenever I hear the song, "He ain't heavy, he's my brother." Except for the "ain't," it's an appropriate song about him.

Besides my poor aching back from pulling my heavily loaded trailer brother, all went well, at least for a while. Until one day *Trailey* decided that he'd had enough and broke a leg. Or a wheel, at least. I felt sorry for Dad and his family. Now they were stranded in the middle of nowhere without food or money. But at least they found a place to stay that night. *Trailey* and I had to sit moping in the pouring rain. Thinking back, despite all the hardships, I am one of the most blessed of cars. And, of course, the toughest.

In photos, those dirt roads might look smooth, but I tell you, they make me bump up and down like crazy. Proof of my bravery is that I once crossed a bridge made of loose planks once when Dad told me to. Those planks really hopped around under me, but hey, we made it. In fact, I've crossed worse, but Dad was too psyched out those times to take photos. Oh, well.

The following secret is really embarrassing, but I will tell you about it. I have also been used as a kind of toilet enclosure. Where there were no gas stations or bathrooms for many miles, the humans say, "if you gotta go, you gotta go." But the humiliation of having to look away while they use *me* to conceal them doing their... business, was almost too much. To my credit, I must say that when both doors on my one side are open, and I'm parked next to high bushes, I make a pretty private shelter.

When you look at the roads I've gone through, you might be mistaken into thinking that I can indeed go anywhere. Unfortunately, the truth is that I can't. I have a shortcoming. I can't swim. I can drive through rivers, but only up to a meter deep. The mighty Zambezi River was too daunting, even for me, so I had to cross by ferry. Quite a few times, in fact. I remember, the early ferries were little more than oil drums strapped together with planks tied on top of the drums for me to park on. They had a motor at the back, but I couldn't talk to it. It only spoke Portuguese. The ferry crossings were pretty scary. No railings around the sides, and getting on and off required my all-wheel drive, because there was no ramp, only a muddy, slippery, steep uphill.

I have lived a great life. Over the years my headlights have seen the incredible beauty of creation, the destruction left by war and many strange—and sometimes amusing—sights.

Traveling down many highways and byways, I have collected some scars, the proof of many bumps and scratches over the years. I have at times, experienced some unplanned, improvised operations to fix some serious medical problems, as a direct result of damaged roads. But, I am happy to say, I have helped people with cholera, malaria, and AIDS, and pregnant mothers get medical help. I have taken people to funerals and have transported others to happier occasions too. I've done all of this for my loved ones out of the kindness of my on-board computer heart.

Even though I am only a car, I am privileged to have seen so much love, heard the peals of laughter, and witnessed the tears of sadness and suffering. I am the better for it.

One could say it is as if I've lived the life of two Toyotas.

There's a white man—and he's walking!

Henry, Mozambique

It was another hot day. I was on my way to see my language helper when I walked past a group of kids kicking around a "ball." By "ball," I mean a bunch of plastic bags tied together with string. When they saw me, they froze and just stared.

I immediately thought, "Did I forget to button up something? Did I step into chicken poo? Do I have a goat tailing me *again*?" Then, not knowing that I understood them, one of them blurted out in Isoni, in complete astonishment:

"Look. A white man—and he's *walking!*"

What? Why would he say that? I spent the rest of the day thinking about that sentence, convinced I might have misunderstood. I mean, I was fairly confident in my Isoni. But had I misunderstood what that kid said?

Suddenly it clicked. There were almost no cars in *ParkingTicket*. People walked everywhere. The only time those kids ever saw white people was in cars driving on the road that passed *ParkingTicket*. In their world, white people *only* drove in cars. Apparently, I was the first white person they had seen walking. Mystery solved.

Fourteen men and a pickup

Henry, Mozambique

How many adult men can you fit into a normal-sized pickup truck? This is not a riddle—it's an actual question. My personal record was fourteen passengers.

The vehicle? A small, standard-sized double-cab pickup with a canopy on the back. I'm convinced that if we hadn't had the canopy on, I could've shattered that record without even trying.

Now, you may ask, "Why on earth would you do that? Isn't it dangerous?" Well, in the Iso culture, the concept of "personal space" is... debatable. We come from an individualistic culture where everyone is his own man, independent and personally responsible for his own future. The Iso culture is group-oriented and participative, a collective society, where people do everything together. They eat together, work together, make decisions together—and when it's time for a funeral, they most definitely attend together.

That's where our pickup truck came in. It had become the unofficial funeral taxi. At funerals, I'd load it up with people, way beyond its capacity, to get the men to the graveyard. With everyone crowded in the truck and on the back, the front part of the truck almost lifted off the ground. The steering wheel felt very light in my hands. I had to go *veeeery* slowly, especially when approaching a turn. When I turned the wheel, the car would very gradually start veering in the direction I was aiming at. After this experience, I could perhaps be considered a suitable candidate for piloting a large oil tanker.

But the best part was the reactions we got from the traffic police. Usually, they'd jump at the smallest chance to fine you or try to get a bribe. But when I drove past with fourteen serious-looking Muslim men packed into one regular pickup, they suddenly discovered a saintly sense of discretion. Not a question, not a glance—just a wave to move along.

That, my friends, was true freedom.

The sixty-six

Henry, Mozambique

As all these things were happening, I carried on working on translating the chronological Bible stories with Zuba and would walk past Zuberi and his friends daily. They became more and more curious as time went by. Eventually, Zuba and I also completed the stories of the Gospels. We were now ready to present the complete Gospel to the Iso people—in their own language.

Once the task was complete, I started meeting with Zuberi's small group of friends and started telling them the stories, starting with the Old Testament. I also started meetings with some other small groups at the same time.

Some groups chased me away, others simply lost interest. Kovu was a dedicated young Muslim who attended the first several Bible lessons. He was in Zuberi's group. He left the group in disgust, rejecting the gospel before he had even heard it properly. You'll hear a bit more about Kovu later. Eventually I was down to one group—Zuberi's ever-diminishing group. As the group grew smaller and smaller, so did my morale. In the end, the group consisted of just Zuberi and me.

After each day's Bible lesson, I learned more about Zuberi's personal history. Due to Mozambique's cruel civil war, many people had not been able to finish school. Zuberi was one of them. He was in his mid- to late twenties and was attending adult high school at night while selling rice from his porch during the day.

Every day I went to tell him a Bible story on his porch, sitting on the ground in the oppressive heat, breathing in dust and fumes from the trucks passing on the road next to his stall. I was very disappointed. After all, I felt I'd given up so much to be there, only to be wasting all my time and effort on just one person. Despite this, I kept putting all my effort and energy into every presentation. I kept telling the Lord that I'd be faithful. Perhaps I was just trying to convince myself.

The end almost came one day, when, as I took in a big breath to make my next dramatic point, I swallowed a fly! I suspect there's no need to explain my feelings at that point. Turmoil! Frustration! I was near to tears. When I got home, I had quite a "talk" with the Lord. But as usual, He won the argument. He encouraged me, and so I continued.

Just a few days after this event, Zuberi suddenly said, "You know, the guys at night school really like these Bible stories." Flustered, I didn't quite know how to respond, but I thought, "You're a Muslim, you're not supposed to evangelize." However, I kept my pose and didn't say anything. I simply kept on teaching him and left him a printout of each day's lesson, just as I had been doing all along.

A few days later, Zuberi told me how his fellow students would wait for him at school every night, each trying to grab that day's Bible teaching printout first. Every day there was an argument about whose turn it was to get it first. And soon after that, some of the students from another language group joined in because they too wanted to hear the Bible stories. Zuberi and other Iso students had to translate it for them. Then the teacher started taking the printouts off him as soon as he arrived. The teacher now wanted to read it before the others did.

I started wondering how many of these adult students there were in his class. I asked him. "Sixty-six," he replied. Shocked at the large size of his class, I asked him, "What school do you go to, Zuberi?" "Oh," he said, "the Islamic school in the nearby town." Then it dawned on me. That teacher was an *Imam*!

This is the kind of thing the Lord does best. He takes our limited efforts and multiplies them many times. Sixty-six times, in my case. I always say, God is the ultimate organizer.

CHAPTER SEVEN

FIRST FRUITS

---◁◈▷---

Baptism on the beach

Henry, Mocambique

After I led Zuberi through all the chronological teachings, he became a follower of Jesus. Even though he expressed a desire to be baptized, he always avoided going through with it. I suspected he was afraid. One day I asked him again. And he said yes—again. Well, this time he really did come and we left for a clean beach in the nearby town.

On the way, the traffic police stopped us, as often happens. This time, however, the officer "found" a "biiiig problem, big problem" with the car's documentation. He wanted to confiscate the car. The problem? The car's documentation did not state that the car had a canopy and a roof carrier. The car's documentation had been valid for six years up to that point, was officially issued by the government, and had been checked by many, many traffic officers.

No matter how much I told him that it was not I who had generated the car's documentation, it was the Transport

Department that had provided us with the documents, he refused to be moved. But of course it was a Friday and they liked to impound cars on Fridays to keep them over the weekend. The "offender" then had to pay extra storage fees in addition to the hefty fine. The "storage fees" were, in fact, stored in their own pockets. Through all of this I managed to keep my cool, praying under my breath. I also understood what was happening on a spiritual level. This was taking place to keep Zuberi away from his baptism.

Eventually, the officer decided to relent by "only" giving me a fine. As he opened his fine book, I told Zuberi in Isoni that this would take a while. The officer looked up, surprised to hear a white man speaking a local language (my entire discourse with him had been in Portuguese). After a moment, without writing anything, he snapped the book shut and told me "Go! Go!" And I did. *Quickly.*

Praise the Lord! Zuberi was baptized with much joy.

Flowers in the desert

Betsy, Mozambique

Before we first moved to Mozambique, I had often thought about our future among the Iso, trying to picture how we would accomplish the seemingly impossible task of reaching them with the gospel. We knew that they were a group of just over 100,000 with very few, if any, believers. The whole idea was somewhat daunting.

One day, as I was thinking about this, the Lord showed me a vision of a semi-arid land. All I could see was a whole lot of barren nothingness. Suddenly, a small, colorful flower in the sand caught my eye. Then, just as abruptly, another colorful flower popped up. Then two over here, five way over there. Before I knew it, the desert was filled with brilliant colors. I felt the Lord encouraging me, saying: "*This* is how it will happen."

It reminded me of Namaqualand in South Africa. Namaqualand is a semi-desert area that once a year, inexplicably explodes with color as millions upon millions of wildflowers appear overnight and out of nowhere.

While we were living with the Iso, I often thought of that vision of the flowers. I kept asking God, "Where are the flowers, Lord?" The vision encouraged me to pray more and to tell more Bible stories.

Zahra, a friend of mine, had heard that we were telling stories to groups of people in *ParkingTicket*, and she wanted to hear them too. The first time, she was hesitant—unsure of what to expect—so she invited me into her house alone, which was unusual in Iso culture. The next time, we sat outside in her yard. Those early lessons didn't go smoothly. There were many distractions, and one woman in her extended family strongly opposed me sharing the stories with Zahra. I almost gave up, but I sensed the Lord urging me to keep going.

We had just finished going through the Old Testament stories, when Zahra told me that she had had a dream. We knew about the many incidences of Muslims having dreams and visions that often led them to Jesus, especially during the time of Ramadan, their fasting month. But for us it always seemed to only happen in faraway places. So when this happened to my friend, I was super excited.

In her dream, Zahra had come to my house and walked through the front gate. When she wanted to leave again, she somehow couldn't go back through the same gate. She had to leave by the back gate. Just outside the back gate was a stairway going up to heaven. She tried climbing up the stairway but couldn't do so on her own. The dream was so similar to Jacob's ladder and Jesus' comment about it (John 1:51) that it was easy for me to explain it to her.

The Lord showed me the significance of her coming in through one gate and leaving through another. It was symbolic of her leaving an old belief system behind and entering a new one. I tried to explain to her that climbing the stairway to heaven was only made possible by Jesus. At that point in time, she couldn't quite understand it. She just wasn't ready—yet.

We carried on with the stories and got to the New Testament. One day, while I was telling her the story of Jesus and Nicodemus (John 3), I could clearly see the light come in her eyes. The truth had dawned on her. She finally understood her dream. She understood that she could never reach God on her own, and that Jesus was the only way. Jesus was the stairway. Jesus was no longer a mere prophet—He was now her *Savior*. Zahra was smitten with Jesus.

Only years later and a long time after this event did we realize that her name, Zahra, meant "flower." She was the first female flower in that barren dessert that God showed me years before.

Soon afterward, we had to go to South Africa again, for a few weeks. We were concerned leaving the two new believers behind: Zuberi, who had come to faith a week before Zahra, were the only two new believers in a village of 10,000 Muslims, and here we were leaving them behind for three weeks. We left them but God didn't.

When we got back from our trip, I immediately went to Zahra's house. One of her sisters saw me first, smiling broadly. After greeting me profusely, she said, "I didn't know that Jesus is the Son of God!" What? I almost swallowed my tongue. Where did she get that? Soon Zahra joined us, telling me that now seven of her family members also believed in Jesus.

While we were away, she had told them all the stories I had told her. She explained to them why she believed that Jesus was her Savior, and that He was the Son of God. This concept is normally a massive obstacle to overcome for Muslims because they have huge misconceptions about what that means. But Zahra knew how to explain it in a way that made sense to her family, and they had all became believers.

I decided right then, if this is what happens when we're away, we should go away more often! Almost overnight, a small fellowship of female believers had been born. Many years after we had left, one of the Bible translators visited *ParkingTicket*. He sent us an email saying that there were three small Christian fellowships in the village now. Attached in the email was a photo of Zahra among other believers, praying for someone. The flowers have started blooming in the desert.

An almost fatal baptism

Betsy, Mozambique

Soon this group of new believers wanted to be baptized. It was Zahra, her two sisters, her sister-in-law, a cousin, a friend who was living with them, and her twelve-year-old son, Bako. We invited them to our house where we showed them the Jesus Film in Isoni and they could also see how John the Baptist baptized Jesus.

Henry and I explained to them what baptism means. Baptism is a huge step for Muslims to take. Still, they were adamant that they wanted to be baptized. I asked Zahra if she wanted to baptize her son. She was *so* excited to do that. We wanted to teach them early on that any believer could baptize a new believer.

We took them all to a clean beach, where we asked each one why they wanted to be baptized. Henry took a video of each one's simple but profound testimony. Then I had the privilege of wading with them into the luke-warm water and baptizing them.

When it came to Bako's turn, Zahra was ecstatic. But the moment was too big for her. She took the boy, had him bowed forward, pushed his head under the water, and said "I baptize you in the name of the Father, and…err…," she thought for a moment, then hesitantly continued"… and in the name of Jesus…" And then she froze. Right at this moment, in her excitement, she had forgotten the rest. But she still held Bako's head under the water.

Bako started squirming, his arms began thrashing about in a panic. This was not good. I grabbed him, pulling him out of the water, shouting, "And in the name of the Holy Spirit!" We almost buried him for real that day. He sure wouldn't forget his baptism. Afterward, we sat together for an hour or more in the shallow, lukewarm water, singing songs about Jesus—songs that *they* had composed. What an experience. I was almost in heaven already. Almost.

Henry was on the beach, filming, when a stranger approached him. As it happened, this man was a South African, doing some contracting work in the area. By chance, he was walking on that beach that day, saw what was happening, and realized that it was a baptism. He was curious, so he approached Henry. It turned out that this man was from our very own church in South Africa. Yes, really! He took a copy of the baptism Henry had filmed back to our church. When the pastor showed the video to the congregation, they erupted in praise! Yet another amazing *God-incidence.*

What does your miracle look like?

Betsy, Mozambique

Living with the Iso people was challenging. Most were illiterate, poor and hungry. Then there was the harsh heat, bad quality food, cholera, malaria... And most didn't know Jesus as their Savior. People were dying all the time, mostly from malaria and malnutrition.

Seeing people suffer was a common sight in our village —suffering from sicknesses, the challenges of life, hopelessness. Whenever I saw little Zaki, it felt like my heart had been ripped out. He was severely disabled—mentally and physically. He couldn't walk since birth. He never learned to speak. He had to slide along the ground on his bottom, sometimes even without pants—a truly heart-breaking sight to behold. His useless legs were as thin as bamboo sticks. And the other kids would make fun of him, too.

The small group of Isoni believers and I began to pray for his healing. Nothing changed. I was confused about this. Why was God silent?

"Before you call I will answer, while you are still speaking, I will hear" (Isaiah 65:24).

What about Matthew 7:7, *"Ask, and it will be given to you"*?

Didn't God hear? Didn't He care?

One day, while the small group of believers were celebrating the Lord's Supper, the women spontaneously began to sing in Isoni,

We won't stop praying until Zaki starts walking!

We won't stop praying until Zaki starts walking!

And then God did it. The next week Zaki had been chosen "at random" for specialized treatment at the local hospital in the nearby town. This was nothing short of a miracle. Again, one of those *God-incidences.*

We watched, we waited, we prayed. A few months later, the seemingly impossible happened. Zaki took his first steps. We were in awe as we watched him smiling and playing with the other children. Although he still was not talking, and he was walking laboriously, it didn't matter. His whole demeanor had changed.

My idea of a miracle up to that point had been an instantaneous healing, a powerful deliverance, a timely breakthrough. Praying for Zaki, I envisioned something similar—him getting up, walking and speaking in an instant, like in the Bible. But God showed us a different way.

Yet I *knew* the circumstances in that village—him being arbitrarily chosen for treatment was a miracle. That was God's answer to our prayers. Miracles come in different forms.

Keep on praying for your miracle, for your breakthrough. And look out—maybe God has answered you already, just in a different way than you expected.

Be joyful in hope, patient in affliction, persistent in prayer (Romans 12:12).

Jesus and the adulteress

Betsy, Mozambique

Most days I was teaching the group of female believers about Jesus, prayer, and everything else. They loved the chronological Bible stories Henry had translated into Isoni with his language helper. We sang the songs that *they* had composed about Jesus, and we had long conversations about life.

One day I was telling them about Jesus and the adulterous woman (John 8). Huddled together, no one talked. This was not like them. The women were mesmerized. What would Jesus do with this adulterous woman?

"'Teacher, this woman was caught in the act of adultery. In the Law Moses commanded us to stone such a woman. So what do You say?' They said this to test Him, in order to have a basis for accusing Him. Jesus bent down and began to write on the ground with His finger" (John 8:4-6).

Adultery was no strange thing among the Iso. Many had been forced to prove their fertility before marriage, only to be abandoned afterward. According to Islamic law, men could marry four wives. This caused jealousy, rivalry, and heartbreak. Some of these women had been mothers since they were still teenagers, with no husband in sight. This story hit close to home.

When I reached the part where Jesus was writing in the sand, I also bent down and wrote in the sand. The kids thought that was fun. They mimicked me and wrote and played in the sand, causing dust clouds and laughter.

When they continued to question Him, He straightened up and said to them, "Let him who is without sin among you be the first to cast a stone at her." And again He bent down and wrote on the ground (John 8:7-8).

More writing in the sand. The women laughed in delight —not in mockery, but joy. Jesus was a man who stood *with* the woman, not against her.

Jesus asked her, "Woman, where are your accusers? Has no one condemned you?" "No one, Lord," she answered. "Then neither do I condemn you," Jesus declared. "Now go and sin no more" (John 8:10-11).

That was *their* Jesus, the Jesus they worshiped. "Tell the story again," they pleaded.

Just then, across the dusty road, a woman named Lila walked by. She was known for her many partners and children with different fathers. Suddenly Zahra shouted loud enough for the world to hear, "*Lila, come listen! This story is for you —you're an adulteress, after all!*"

My face went red with embarrassment, waiting for an argument to break out. But Lila brazenly walked over to where we were sitting on the side of the road. Now everyone tried to tell her the story. I could get a word in here and there, correcting them where they got it wrong. The kids were writing in the sand, dust everywhere. Lila listened quietly, and after the story was finished, she just got up and went home.

A few months later Zahra came to me, excitingly telling me about an upcoming wedding. Weddings were a big event in *ParkingTicket*—everyone, I mean the whole neighborhood went. It could go on for days. There would be food for all, and it was usually a time to have fun and just forget about the hardships of life. I loved those ceremonies, and excitedly I asked her whose wedding it was. "It's Lila's," she told me with a big smile.

Of course Zahra filled me in with all the juicy gossip: After Lila heard the story of Jesus and the adulterous woman, she started to become very aware of her way of life and the choices she had made. Even though she was not a believer then, the Holy Spirit had started to convict her. She told her partner the Bible story and they decided that living together was not pleasing to God. Therefore, they decided to get married.

The story of the adulterous woman became the Iso women's all-time favorite. And for me, that day remains one of my most treasured memories I have of all my years of living in *ParkingTicket*.

This is why Bible storytelling is so powerful—it draws listeners in and makes them feel part of the story, which leaves a lasting emotional impact. And then the discussions afterward make each story memorable. Bible stories convey spiritual truths in a simple way people can understand, remember, and pass on to others—even if they can't read.

Slow learner

Betsy, Mozambique

Every morning, as I prepared to go out, I would put on my headscarf and would tell God that I would not go out of the house unless He went with me. I knew He promised in His Word that He would always be with me, and I trusted that He would be faithful to His Word.

I just needed to hear myself saying that.

Life in *ParkingTicket*—where salty, humid air carried the smells of drying fish, cooking fires, and garbage heaps, and where poverty and illness were constant companions—taught me how utterly dependent I was on God. I was so thankful for all His blessings in my life.

The days were steaming hot. Early mornings were the only time that the heat was still manageable. I could visit Zahra and the group of female believers and be back in time to make lunch—well, most days. Between noon and three in the afternoon, the streets emptied out and no living soul could be seen. For good reason. It was simply too hot to do anything, except doze off in the shade. Only a few courageous chickens would brave the heat and could sometimes be found rummaging through the garbage heaps next to the road.

At that point we only had a partial print of the first five books of the Bible (the Taureti)—not that it helped much, because the villagers were all functionally illiterate. They were oral learners. That means that what they were learning about God and Jesus had to come from my mouth, and later on, from the recordings we would make.

In the process, I learned patience, with a capital P, when meeting with the women. Some days, an hour could easily pass before we even started talking about Jesus. Interruptions were the biggest event of the day. The fish mongers would often come by just as everyone had finally arrived and were sitting together. Everything had to stop until they had bargained the best price for a few fish. Or, they had to hang up their washing first because it had rained the previous day, or someone was sick and needed to go to the clinic, or a baby was born the previous night, or... you catch my drift.

That day, just like any other, the believing women slowly got together. Sitting on a straw mat in the shade, they started singing songs about Jesus. And then a Muslim funeral procession went by. Usually, these processions were led by a hearse of some sort—usually someone's truck that they borrowed, and on the back of the truck was the homemade casket. Another few trucks, with the men standing on the back of the trucks, would follow. These trucks were packed with men, holding onto each other so as not to fall off. As the older men wanted to get on, the younger ones would be thrown off. Yes, I saw it with my own eyes. Our small pick-up truck was often part of the procession, with Henry as the driver, packed to the hilt with Muslim men.

As solemn as the situation was, I thought to ask the believers a question, using the funeral as the topic for a lesson. "That man who died, where is he now?," I asked.

"His body is going into the ground, but his spirit is with God," Zahra replied confidently, and the others agreed.

I was devastated. After *a year* of teachings and daily intense discussions, they still did not understand. What did they really believe? Had they not been baptized into the Name of Jesus, and professed that He was the only way to heaven (John 14:6 and Acts 4:12)?

I hoped that Zahra had perhaps just not understood my question, so I asked again where the dead man was. She replied with the same answer, this time slightly more animated. I asked her why she said he was with God. Trying to suppress her irritation with my slowness of understanding, Zahra took me by the shoulders and replied impatiently, "Because he believed Jesus was his Savior, just as we do."

151

I was stunned! Most of the people in the village were Muslim, and I thought I pretty much knew all the believers.

"But how do you know he believed in Jesus?" I asked. Then she told me the story of the unknown fisherman who became a Jesus-follower:

Zahra had a small TV, video player and a generator. She showed movies in her backyard at night, charging the movie goers a few cents. Usually they watched dubbed-over action movies, or movies about superstitious events and ghosts. A while ago, I decided to give her our copy of the old movie "The Ten Commandments." It was a *great* hit. But I wondered how they understood what was going on because this movie was in English. She explained, very patiently, that while the movie was playing, she would provide an impromptu translation into Isoni. She said, "I know all these stories; I just tell them what's happening." Way to go, Zahra!

We eventually had the Jesus Film translated into Isoni too, so I eagerly gave her a copy. She started showing it at night to the neighbors. One evening, this fisherman came to watch the Jesus movie. Afterward, he stayed behind, lingering in the yard until everybody had gone. He started asking Zahra questions about this Jesus he had seen in the movie. She explained to him about Jesus and the atonement. And later that night he told her that he also believed in Jesus. This was the man whose funeral procession we were watching.

"So," she said, looking at me intently, "*that* is why I am telling you that his body is going into the ground, but his spirit is with God."

"If you declare with your mouth, 'Jesus is Lord,' and believe in your heart that God raised him from the dead, you will be saved" (Romans 10:9).

The seeds are bearing healing fruit

Henry, Mozambique

As a new believer, Asani was very excited because the first time he had prayed for someone other than his own family, he had seen God heal the person miraculously. A lady in his neighborhood had been screaming all morning and seemed to be possessed by some evil spirit or illness. Many others had come into her yard to try to calm her down but had eventually given up and left.

Asani visited her and started praying out loud in the name of Jesus. Although she didn't calm down immediately, he didn't give up and continued praying. After about fifteen minutes, she suddenly quietened down, sat up and soon started eating. We encouraged him to go back and visit her and share the news about who Jesus is with her and her family.

When the light is green, the cars go

Henry, Mozambique

I walked to the market in *ParkingTicket* one day, as I often did, when I stumbled onto a lively discussion among a group of men. The topic? Not politics, not malaria, not even the price of onions. No, they were talking about the technological progress in the nearest city. A set of traffic lights had been installed there!

To them, the city was like another planet—500 km away (300 miles). Most of them had never even been further than the nearby town, which was walking distance away from *ParkingTicket*. Now, they all were confronted with a daunting question—what on earth would they do if they ever went to the "big city" and came to one of these newfangled traffic lights?

One of them was getting quite anxious about this. Then another guy decided to quell this man's fears. His chest swelled with pride. After all, he had been to that city and to a couple of neighboring islands too. A veritable world traveler, wise and knowledgeable.

"It's very simple," he said as a matter of fact and with great confidence. "When the light is green, the cars go. When the light is red, the people go." Errrr...oops... I felt I had to interject at this point to avert a serious accident in the future.

This just goes to show you how a destructive, devastating civil war can hold people back and stifle progress.

Money matters

Betsy, Mozambique

"*Nu Beti*[17], what do you have in your bag?," the old mama yelled from her house as I walked past. How rude, I thought.

I was coming home from the little market in our village. The heat was brutal. I'm sure the only thing standing between Isoland and the sun was a thin piece of rusted corrugated iron. I had my head scarf on and a cloth around my waist. Looked like a real Iso woman.

"Some onions, bananas and rice," I reluctantly revealed my purchases.

"What did you pay?"

Really? This is wrong. I am sure the whole world knows that you do not ask such private questions, especially when it

17 "Older Sister Betsy" is a respect form in Isoni

comes to money. Knowing a bit how things work around here, I relented.

"Twenty Meticais," I said reluctantly. Is this a form of interrogation?

"What? You paid too much. Give me some!," she yelled out loudly. Great. Now everybody knows. It was obvious to me that I was not a real Iso yet.

Talking about money is a taboo in many cultures. In some Western cultures, you can hardly allow yourself to even *think* about someone else's salary, let alone ask. What you paid for your new computer or shoes, even what you were charged for your dental check-up is off-limits in any conversation. You can release some of the "curiosity pressure" about your new phone or blouse by saying you got it "on a special," a discounted price.

It is not really lying. The price was very special to you.

In other cultures, they almost have a fun relationship with money—especially in informal markets. In Thailand, for example, you are expected to bargain for the price of that fake T-shirt or silk handbag you want to buy. It is like a game.

I got right into that when we went to Thailand for a conference. Henry couldn't believe what he was seeing—his somewhat shy wife had turned into a negotiation monster, arguing and laughing with the sellers, using the calculator as a weapon—and a translation device. Numbers are numbers in any language. He thanked me later. I got that genuine imitation silk scarf for far less than half of the original price.

Soon afterward, we had to travel to Singapore. In a shiny, spotless mall, I spotted a small stand selling shirts—and immediately, my heart started to race. Bargaining opportunity! My hard-earned experience had taught me the golden rule:

start small. First, ask the price of one item. Then, casually inquire about the price for two or more. That's when the magic happens—the real bargaining begins. The game was on.

I asked the lady what the price was for one shirt. "Five dollars." Good, I was going in for the kill. I almost giggled to myself. This is fun. "How much for two shirts?," I asked, enjoying my own cleverness.

She looked at me for a long time with a kind of sarcastic look on her face. I almost saw pity there too.

"Ten dollars," she replied slowly, not adding the implied "idiot!" One shirt is five dollars. Then two should be ten.

With a red face, and Henry trying to keep up while in a fit of laughter, I walked out of the mall very quickly. No looking back. I am sure if I did, I would have seen her standing there in disbelief, trying to work out how anybody could be so dumb. I learned the hard way that there is no bargaining in the malls in Singapore.

Back in *ParkingTicket...* My neighbor Ani and I were funeral buddies, so to speak. We always went to funerals together. While the men are at the grave, the women would sit together in the yard, wailing loudly, hopelessly. It was heart-rending to see them grieving this way. I never got used to it. Someone from the deceased's family would always bring a piece of cloth to the mourning women. Everybody would put in a coin of a certain value. This money would cover some of the funeral expenses.

The unspoken rule was that I always "sponsored" Ani with the funeral money. During one particular funeral I wanted to be generous, and I gave Ani a coin worth five times the expected amount. When the woman came around with the cloth, we threw in our coins. To my absolute horror, I watched as she took out four coins as change.

Nobody blinked an eye. I blinked a few times, though, trying to be nonchalant and Iso-like. For Ani, it was just a matter of opportunity. I couldn't help wondering what the reaction of the people in church in South Africa would be if I were to put in a large note into the collection plate or bag, and then take out some change.

A few years later Henry and I were walking to the Sheikh's house for a visit. A friend of mine was walking the opposite direction. She had a huge bundle on her head.

"Zina, what do you have in your bag?," I shouted in a shrill Iso voice.

"Flour," she shrilled back.

"What did you pay?," I shouted.

Henry just shook his head and smiled.

Coconuts and the Passion of Christ

Betsy, Mozambique

Across Africa and Asia, the coconut tree is known as the "Tree of life." It sounds Biblical, right? And indeed, everything from this tree is useful. Its leaves become roofing, its shells become ladles, fire carriers, or even toy boats for children. The husks are used in mattresses, and some tribes even use them for clothing. Its milk flavors rice, its flesh is eaten. For those who are sick or dehydrated, coconut water revives the body, replenishing lost electrolytes and strengthening the weak. Coconut oil nourishes skin and hair. From root to fruit, nothing is wasted.

To open a coconut, you must strike it hard with a machete or iron rod on a certain spot on the shell to make it crack right around. Then you can separate the two halves by just pulling them apart. Inside a coconut is the most refreshing watery fluid, and white flesh you can scoop out with a spoon.

In many places in Asia and Africa, believers use the coconut to serve as the elements for communion. This is what the Iso believers did too. How fitting that you begin by striking the coconut so the fluid bleeds out.

"The Lord Jesus, on the night He was betrayed, took bread, and when He had given thanks, He broke it and said, 'This is my body, which is for you; do this in remembrance of Me'" (1 Corinthians 11:23–24).

The coconut is struck, broken open, its white flesh eaten with a spoon.

"This cup is the new covenant in My blood; do this, as often as you drink it, in remembrance of Me" (1 Corinthians 11:25).

The coconut's fluid is poured into a cup and shared among the believers present. The symbolism of the blood and the flesh is apparent to everyone.

For the Iso women, sharing communion in this way was simple, beautiful, and their very own. In their Muslim village, alcohol was unavailable, and even juice was costly and hard to come by. But *everybody* had coconuts. With nothing foreign or imported, they could remember together the *"precious blood of Christ, the sinless, spotless Lamb of God"* (1 Peter 1:19).

One day, as we were preparing to have communion, one of the women beside me, expertly cracked open a coconut. This one was brimming with coconut water, and as it split open, some of the fluid splattered onto me. At that moment, a scene in the movie *The Passion of the Christ* flashed through my mind. It was the moment when the soldiers flogged Jesus until His blood splattered across their garments and faces. Suddenly, the coconut water that splashed on my skin was no longer just coconut water—this became a powerful reminder of His sacrifice. My heart cried out, "*I* crucified Jesus! *I* crucified Jesus!"

I struggled to compose myself, for in that moment I knew: this was communion in its truest sense. Not a Sunday morning ritual, but a raw, living remembrance of the One broken for me.

CHAPTER EIGHT

JESUS SPEAKS ISONI

---·◅⊙⊙⊙▻·---

Using technology to reproduce

Henry, Mozambique

It soon became clear that the two of us, with the few Iso believers, were not sufficient to spread the gospel far and wide. The Iso were mostly illiterate, so we couldn't use printed material. (This was before the Disciple Making Movement approach became widely understood.)

As my background was in software engineering, I loved anything technological. God knew that. That's why He put me there at the right moment, knowing that I would just love a technical challenge like this.

We decided to record all the chronological Bible stories and Scripture portions that had been translated at that time and put them on electronic players so people could listen to the recordings. After all, Romans 10:17 states that faith comes from *hearing* the word of Christ. With this in mind, we endeavored to build a makeshift audio recording studio in our home.

Them gospel glues

Henry, Mozambique

No, the title is *not* a typo! The question is, how many dabs of glue does it take to assemble enough egg cartons to soundproof the room where the Isoni Bible stories are to be recorded? Well, let's see, two layers of cartons, times 387 cartons to cover the walls and the ceiling, times forty-two bumps on each—32,508 glue dots!

The first challenge—where would we find that many egg cartons in a place where you couldn't even buy commercial eggs? The only eggs available in our area were from someone's backyard chickens, laid wherever they pleased. We heard about a chicken farmer about 500 km away who graciously decided to donate all the egg cartons we needed. Check!

That's only part of the challenge that lay before the team of seven people that had driven in convoy with us from South Africa. Their objective was to convert our son's old bedroom, seeing that he was now in boarding school in South Africa, into a makeshift recording studio.

The visiting team had to travel around 6,600 km (4,125 miles) by car; braving rain, mud, customs officials, corrupt traffic officers, and a mile-wide river crossing by ferry. Just getting to *ParkingTicket* took the team five days. Only then did their real work start. But they did it. Check.

The egg cartons had to be glued to something. But what? So they built bamboo frames. Some started gluing the egg cartons, while the rest of the team built the frames. Next came the electrical wiring that had to be done. More egg cartons glued together. The completed bamboo frames were put in place. Egg cartons glued. After a lot of sweat, and not a lot of tears, (it's permanently summer in the tropics), we were done!

Of course it wasn't all hard toil and sweat' We showed them some beautiful locations, parts of God's incredible creation, along the way. We swam in the sea and laughed our heads off at everyone's hilarious jokes and antics. What teamwork. Oh, and we used about four liters of glue.

Through it all, there were no complaints about the heat, the insect bites, the long hours, etc. What a humbling privilege it was for us to have such an awesome team come all that way to visit us and enable us to carry on with the work that God had given us. We were now able to produce broadcast quality audio recordings right there in Isoland!

People from all over the world supported the project: Funds for the recording equipment came from Singapore, people from our home church in South Africa paid for all the materials, and each person in the team raised the necessary financial support to cover their own travel and lodging expenses.

After some time, other missionaries heard about our "studio" and came to see what we were doing and how they could also do something similar. Most of them made comments like "This is amazing," or "What a good idea it is to record Bible lessons for illiterate people." Some asked technical questions.

But this one woman showed remarkable insight. She didn't say a word during the demonstration. When the conversation died down, she came up with a profound statement that I'll never forget. She said, "Wow, you must have eaten a lot of eggs." Well said, oh wise one.

No problem

Henry, Mozambique

We had our recording studio. The next challenge was to find an Iso who could help with the recordings. We knew we had to use a native speaker to make the recordings not sound foreign. We also knew it would be better to use a man rather than a woman, because of cultural issues. We preferred that the narrator should be a believer. But where would we find an Iso man who can read well, has a good voice, *and* is a believer? At that time, we knew of only three Iso male believers, and two were busy helping the Bible translators.

Thankfully Zuberi was willing. The strange thing though was that while he could read Portuguese well, he couldn't read his own language Isoni. I knew another Iso man called Badru, who was very clever. He spoke a few of the local languages, but… he wasn't a believer yet, and he had a speech problem. However, he could be a good checker because he taught himself to read Isoni. I could read Isoni well enough but I may sometimes get the tone[18] wrong and might change the meaning of a word without realizing it.

So, this is how we did it: I would read a short part of the text, usually not even an entire sentence. For example, I would read, "In the beginning," and Zuberi, the narrator, repeated it. I would read it again and click the record button. Zuberi would say it again, speaking into the microphone. Badru sat next to me, constantly checking for pronunciation or tonal errors or even missing words. Isoni is complicated and it's all too easy to make mistakes. If Badru gave the nod, I would go on to the next phrase. "God made the heavens and the earth."

18 Isoni is a tonal language where the meaning of words can change based on the pitch or tone used when pronouncing them.

Twice again, recording it the second time. Using this method we ended up with hundreds of short fragments of recorded audio.

Once we had done this for two hours or so, we were all tired. After they left, I would transfer the recorded files onto the computer. There I merged all the recorded bits together. Unfortunately, there was a slight problem. Every time I pressed the record button in the studio, you could hear an audible "click" on the recording. There were hundreds of clicks. Betsy had to patiently use audio editing software to remove each click from the merged audio, and to put consistent pauses between commas and sentences. It was a very slow and tedious process, but we could find no other way.

Every morning we would complete two hours of recording—*if* we had electricity, and *if* both men arrived. Next came four to five hours of editing. The result was a product that was broadcast quality, sounding natural enough. We once estimated that for an hour's recording, we had put in about twenty hours of work.

Why would we go through all this trouble? Because: *"... how then can they call on the One in whom they have not believed? And how can they believe in the One of whom they have not heard? And how can they hear without someone to preach?"* (Romans 10:14).

Frightened into faith

Henry, Mozambique

One day, after we had been recording the chronological Bible teachings and parts of the Bible for over a year and were making good progress, Badru suddenly disappeared. I needed another checker. Enter Kovu, the dedicated Muslim who had been in Zuberi's group and who had rejected the gospel.

Kovu was a Quranic teacher—devout, intelligent, and literate. As I mentioned earlier, he had once joined Zuberi in listening to the Bible stories but had left the group in anger. Still, we had managed to stay on friendly terms. I'll admit, I had some doubts about the wisdom of involving him in recording the Bible stories. Yet I couldn't shake the sense that God had a purpose in it. So I asked if he would help us, and he readily agreed. We paid for the work, of course, so perhaps the money was the main motivation.

Things went smoothly. He was a really good checker. Better than Badru, in fact. After some time, he started to become interested in what we were recording. We soon started recording the book of Revelation. I could see his eyes getting bigger when we read about some of the end-time judgments. It must have startled him, because he started asking questions about what we were recording. He soon had my head working in overdrive, trying to explain difficult concepts from Revelation to him, in Isoni.

I would occasionally ask him, "Who is Jesus to you?" This was a tip I got from an Ethiopian missionary. In many cultures where older people are respected, people would often answer your questions the way they think you would prefer to have them answered. In such shame-driven cultures, they don't want to offend you with an answer you might not like, they want to honor you. So, if you were to ask someone from such a culture whether they believe in Jesus, they might say "yes" out of respect for you.

Asking open questions to get people to think, is how Jesus taught. For example in Matthew 16:13-16 Jesus asks his disciples, "Who do the people say the Son of Man is?" and "Who do *you* say I am?" Because these are not leading questions, you will most probably get a completely honest answer.

When I asked Kovu, "Who is Jesus to you?," I would get the standard Muslim answer: "He is a prophet." I didn't comment on this, I simply continued answering his questions about Revelation. From time to time, I would ask him this again, hoping that the explanations about the Bible were making a difference. One day, after asking him who Jesus was to him, he replied: "Jesus is a great prophet, and he's the Messiah." Yes! Progress. I could see he was gradually growing in his understanding of Jesus. He got really scared about certain sections of Revelation, and his questions became more and more heartfelt and sincere.

Again, later on I asked him, "Who is Jesus to you?" He replied, "He is a great prophet, and the Messiah." I was getting despondent. Is he ever going to get it? He started walking toward our gate and stopped in his tracks, thinking for a moment. Then he turned around and said, "And He is my Savior." I almost *exploded* with joy. I never thought that the book of Revelation could be used in evangelism.

The two men from the island (continued)

Henry, Mozambique

You may remember, at the beginning of the book, I mentioned the incident about the two intimidating strangers in Islamic garb that appeared at our door early one morning. This is the rest of that story. Let me start at the beginning again.

When I opened our front door, my heart skipped a beat. Even though it was still early in the morning, the air was thick with the unrelenting tropical heat. In the distance, I could faintly hear the sound of fishermen calling out to their helpers and the thumping sound of women pounding their rice.

Before me stood two big strangers. They wore full Islamic garb—spotless white robes reaching their ankles, Muslim prayer beads in their hands, gofia[19] caps set firmly on their heads. They looked very solemn. I could tell this was about something very serious and important.

"This is trouble," I thought, knowing that only the strict Imams[20] dressed like that—and never when they came to visit me.

At that moment, a jumble of thoughts popped into my head: What am I even doing here? How did I ever manage to get myself into this situation?

Sometime before this incident, I had given Kovu one of the MP3 players with the recordings of the Bible lessons. He loved playing the gospel teachings to whomever would listen. He often visited a certain tiny island, and he played the teaching for the people there. He told me that one of the men just couldn't get enough of these teachings. He had listened to them over and over again. He begged me to get this man his own MP3 player, and I eventually relented. I was always cautious not to hand the players just to anyone. We had limited supplies.

One day, Kovu told me that this man from the island wanted to come and see me. Even after listening to the teachings for months, this man still had a burning question he wanted to ask me. I thought to myself, "really?" After all those hours and hours of recorded teachings and Bible stories,

19 Cap worn by Muslim men
20 Islamic leaders

how could there still be something we had not explained clearly? Had we forgotten some important theological truth? We had truly tried to think of and cover all the important Christian truths in our teachings. What could be missing?

Kovu had also mentioned to the man that the Jesus video was available in Isoni and he wanted to watch it. I told Kovu that he could bring the man from the island to see me. Then he could ask his question and watch the movie.

I had been expecting Kovu and this man from the island to arrive together. Island people normally did not dress elaborately or smartly. The last thing I expected to see was two formally dressed strangers on my doorstep. And Kovu wasn't with them. However I cautiously invited them in.

The older one of the two immediately started bubbling over with enthusiasm. He said that he was so excited to see the video about Jesus, because through the Bible stories he and the people of his village had come to love Jesus and to follow His teachings. Apparently, this man was the small island's Islamic leader. As you might imagine, my heart jumped for joy. I let him chatter on for a while, enjoying the moment.

Eventually I plucked up the courage to ask him what his question was. I was nervous because I thought that it might be some difficult or controversial theological question about something in the teachings, something I might not be able to explain well or answer.

The moment for the question came. He looked me right in the eye, and asked, "What does a cross look like?"

This was the big question? What does a cross look like? Out of *all* the possible questions he could have asked. I was shocked and more than a little surprised. I had always assumed that surely *everybody* in the world would know what a cross looks like. I realized that I had never explained the cross in the teachings. To be honest, it had never even come to mind.

I told him and his friend to sit down and watch the Jesus video with me, then they would see what a cross looks like.

The first moment Jesus came onto the screen of my computer, his face lit up. He said, "Yes, this is the Jesus I love!" He enthusiastically agreed aloud with every word Jesus said. It was almost as if he was cheering Jesus on. And toward the end of the movie, he finally learned what a cross looked like.

Thinking back on this incident, I realized anew what an Unreached People Group is really like. They have never had the opportunity to hear the Good News about Jesus—not even in the least bit. But now these people from a small remote island had. God is good and faithful.

I'm rude now—and loving it!

Betsy, Mozambique

Eating rice and beans on most days was just one of the many new customs we had to adapt to when we moved to the Iso. The culture shock comes after a few months in, and then reverse culture stress when you go back home. This phenomenon is well-known to all people who live cross-culturally. We were not spared from this initiation into our new existence. It meant going through a painful period of adaptation and learning to "live and let live" in a culture which was not our own. In spiritual terms, we had to die to ourselves.

There were many challenges, yet living with the Iso made me feel alive, full of purpose and most of all, totally dependent on God.

One of the first things I learned was that I could be real. What a novelty. I could tell people if I didn't feel well, and exactly what was wrong—not just the normal, "Hi-how-are-you-I-am-well-thank you" ritual.

I could walk barefoot between the straw-roofed mud huts if I wanted to, and on occasion, I danced with some of my friends in the sand-street alleys during celebrations. I was free to greet everyone, because I knew everyone would greet me back. Then would follow the expected questions about our respective family's health, which could be quite detailed—depending on the size of the family. And then some more "why, what, why and how..."

Our perspectives on personal space—the physical personal distance people prefer—are influenced by our own culture. Unfortunately, the invisible "rules" of personal space become evident only when you violate them.

The Iso were very comfortable with little personal space—they could be very close to other people all the time. I had to get used to having people sit right up against me, half-way on top of me, children playing with my hair and constantly pulling the hair on my arms, and my girlfriends holding my hand when walking down the street.

This cultural assault on the senses was overwhelming, but worthwhile. To be able to sit most days on a straw mat with a small group of Iso female believers, while teaching them in their own heart language and enjoying Jesus' presence with them, was precious. Despite my longing for my kids far away, the heat, the flies, the mosquitoes and the sweat trickling down my back, all vying for my attention, my heart silently screamed with joy:

THIS IS WHAT I WAS BORN FOR.

The biggest challenge I had to overcome though, were the blunt comments on my "full figure."

"What are you eating?" *"You are really getting fat now."*

Since we had come to live with the Iso, the change in diet there had also changed my figure. The last thing I wanted to hear was the dreaded "FAT" comments, which just added insult to injury.

"Wow, you became really fat since I last saw you."— which, incidentally, was the day before!

I soon came to understand that comments like those were intended to be BIG complements (yes, that is a pun). Being fat, for them, meant that I was prosperous and healthy. In many African cultures, fuller figures are a sign of good health. Praise the Lord! This cultural belief makes sense, because many of these countries are coming out of wars. Malnutrition and diseases like cholera are endemic. Many Iso are thin, and they try everything to look fat—even going to the length of putting on many layers of clothing, despite the tropical heat. Being skinny, or losing weight, was a sign of sickness or hardship.

I slowly changed in this respect—my mindset, that is, not my weight!

For many missionaries, visiting their home country means adapting back into their own culture. This can be accompanied by reverse culture shock, which can often be worse than the initial cultural shock when entering a foreign culture. This was true for us too. One missionary summed it up succinctly, saying that she "felt like a foreigner in her own country."

But I often giggled silently to myself when visiting home. What would a friend think if I were to tell her that she had really become fat since I last saw her? Or if I asked an ex-colleague what salary he earned? Or, if I told my mother-in-law that her new sofa was ugly?

I came to the conclusion that the solution to this challenge was to become like a chameleon. When among the Iso, I could be rude and love it, but back home I needed to adapt to a more subtle shade of inquisitiveness.

Never underestimate a child

Betsy, Mozambique

After Zahra became a Follower of Jesus, she led her fifteen-year-old son, Bako, to the Lord. Bako wanted one of the solar-powered players with the Bible stories on it. He told us that he wanted to play the stories to his friends. We were a bit hesitant to give him one, because owning one could cause envy between him and his friends, or even be used as a status symbol instead of a gospel tool. After praying about the matter, we felt satisfied that we should do it.

Henry taught him how to use the little machine, and we insisted that he pause the player after each of the questions that came at the end of each lesson. He was to wait for the kids to answer the questions before moving on to the next lesson. This would force them to think about what they were listening to. So off he went, grinning like he'd just been given a brand-new boat... except it was a small solar-powered device that taught the gospel.

A few days later, I was visiting friends when, from somewhere, I heard *that voice*—the unmistakable sound of Zuberi's voice on our recordings. Like a bloodhound, I followed the voice through the maze of mud huts until I stumbled upon a surprising sight. Here was Bako, little Bako, sitting in the middle of a group of big and strong Muslim fishermen, all listening so intently to the stories that they didn't even see me or greet me. In this culture, that's basically like ignoring someone standing in your living room. I quietly left.

Later, I asked Bako about it. He just smiled and said, "Oh yes, I've been playing the lessons to the fishermen. And I only let them listen to *one* lesson at a time. Then I play the questions. They must answer the questions before I'll play the next one. That makes them think."

Wow! I was stunned. This little barely-literate teen had not only become an evangelist—he'd turned into a *Bible boot camp instructor.* For years we had prayed for the gospel to spread, to be carried by the Iso people themselves. We just didn't expect a spark to come from a small fifteen-year-old boy with minimal reading skills, but apparently with a master's degree in strategy, and courage to spare.

"Don't let anyone look down on you because you are young, but set an example for the believers in speech, in conduct, in love, in faith and in purity" (1 Timothy 4:12).

Who died?

Henry, Mozambique

Asani came running into our yard, sweating and out of breath. My first thought was: "crisis!" Muslim men always try to be dignified. They will never run unless something is terribly wrong.

"Who died?," I asked him. He laughed as he tried to catch his breath. Nobody died. This was more of a technical crisis.

Asani had one of our early MP3 players that we had been distributing among the Iso. On it was all the chronological Bible lessons we had recorded. At that point we had more than a hundred hours of recordings. As soon as we recorded more, we would ask the ones who had players to bring them back so we could reload the latest teachings on them. The early players needed batteries, and sometime later, we were able to get batteries that charged using a built-in solar panel.

Most of the people couldn't afford batteries. We knew that, so we used rechargeable batteries. But as they didn't have electricity and chargers, we had to charge the batteries for them. We had two truck batteries in our living room that we could use to charge their batteries even when there was no electricity. It made a nice decorating focal point, too. As soon as their batteries died, they would come to us and exchange those for fresh batteries. That was good, because it gave us an indication of who was really listening to the teachings.

Now, the Iso have huge weddings. Muslims from all over would come to these weddings, which could easily last for three days. It was at just such an extended wedding that Asani, who at that point was not a believer yet, decided he would play the recordings. And his plan worked.

A large group of people had been listening for hours, hearing about God, sin and the Messiah in their own language. And then... disaster struck. The batteries died! The group was upset, they were enjoying these teachings, wanting to know more. Because of that, Asani had to run. I quickly gave him fresh batteries, and off he ran back to the wedding.

Afterward he told me what went down. "We would listen to a teaching," he said, "then we would argue for an hour or so. Then we would listen to the same the teaching again and argue some more. After that, we would listen to the next teaching."

He also told me that his cousin from a nearby village was begging him for a MP3 player after hearing some of the teachings at the wedding. I was cautious when handing out a player. We couldn't just give one to anyone because we had a limited supply, so I lent him one. So off Asani went to his cousin's village with a loaded MP3 player.

Weeks later, he told me a story that shook me. Once his cousin started listening to these teachings, he couldn't stop; not for eating, not for sleeping. He listened right through the night. He couldn't get enough. Then, the cousin died a few days after he returned the player.

I believe God spared that man's life just long enough so that he could hear the truth about the Jesus—and that he had accepted Jesus as his savior before his final breath.

The tree and the birds

Henry, Mozambique

The people on the small, isolated island were in bondage to fear. Despite the fact that they were Muslims, they were worshiping the large tree and some kinds of birds on their tiny island. They lived in fear of the spirits living in the tree and in the birds. They believed that these spirits controlled their lives, their safety, their food supply, and their fertility.

One day, a man from the village, Abu, went back to the island after visiting the city. With him he had a small machine that could speak clear Isoni, the language of their hearts. As they listened to the Word of God, they learned that God was greater than any evil spirits. He had created everything. He loved even the people of the island.

The islanders eagerly listened to the teachings. They made a decision to stop worshiping the tree and the birds and started worshiping God. *"Let them give glory unto the LORD, and declare his praise in the islands"* (Isaiah 42:12). How did the Word of God find their way to this small island? This is a story in itself...

Again, it was Kovu who was instrumental in taking the teachings to the island. He introduced me to Abu who commuted back and forth between the island and *ParkingTicket.* He told me how the people on his island worshiped the tree and birds. Abu was convinced that if his people were to hear the Word of God, they would stop doing this. So off he went with Kovu's MP3 player and a small loudspeaker. About three weeks later he was back to tell us what had happened. More batteries and off he went again.

Initially, these people heard only the Old Testament stories. As we recorded more and more, they eventually got to hear the Good News of Jesus.

"My righteousness draws near, My salvation is on the way, and My arms will bring justice to the nations. The islands will look for Me and wait in hope for My arm" (Isaiah 51:5).

CHAPTER NINE

BITS AND PIECES

---⊙⊗⊙---

Afrikaans is the heavenly language

Henry, Mozambique

I was sick with some tropical bug. My whole body ached. My head hurt, and I needed a bed. I was walking home through the thick sandy streets of *ParkingTicket*. Every step felt like I was wading through thick mud, while someone was hitting my head with a hammer.

Two little girls stopped me along the way to proudly recite the Islamic *shahada*[21] in Arabic. I knew what it meant, but I asked them anyway. They didn't know. They just knew the words by heart. I just managed a smile and stumbled on.

When I came to the house of some of our good Iso friends where a little house church was emerging, I *knew* I couldn't just walk past. They would know. Everybody knew everything about everyone in that village. They are very hospitable people, from a group-oriented participative culture. They value friendships deeply.

21　The Shahada is the Islamic declaration of faith, stating, "There is no god but God, and Muhammad is the Messenger of God."

But I was just focused on getting to my bed, drinking some cool water and sleeping. I was really feeling miserable.

Regardless, I went into their yard, hoping just to say a quick hello and goodbye. I should have known by then, it doesn't work like that there. Inside their enclosed yard, it looked like a scene from a disaster movie. People were lying around on mats or sitting against the walls of the their mud huts. Some were sleeping. They scarcely noticed me. This was not normal.

Then Zahra saw me and weakly invited me to come and sit down. They all had some bug—possibly the same one I had. The whole extended family was sick. They didn't offer me water, like they usually do. Nobody talked. I wanted to pray for them, but my head was not working properly either. My tongue felt an inch thick. I just couldn't think in Isoni. Or Portuguese for that matter.

Yet I offered to pray for them. How could I not? I explained that my head hurt too much to speak Isoni, so I would just pray in Afrikaans. I explained to them that God created all the languages, and we could talk to Him in any language. With God's help I prayed for healing for them all in Afrikaans, and stumbled home. Water. Bed. Sleep.

Early the next morning they were all at our door. They looked well, even energetic and joyful. They were all healed. Now they wanted to learn Afrikaans. Because they got healed when I prayed in Afrikaans, Afrikaans must be a powerful language.

I was glad they were healed, but more than a little frustrated because they mistook my Afrikaans language as having more persuasive power with God than Isoni. Didn't I explain it clearly to them? They had seen healings before, where we prayed in Isoni. Thankfully I was feeling better too, so I had more brain power and my Isoni came back. I was able to fully explain to them what happened. And that Afrikaans was nothing special.

I reminded them how they had once prayed for me in Isoni, and God had healed me of malaria. That worked. They understood that it was God who heals, not words spoken in a foreign language.

God's shock treatment

Henry, Mozambique

"What's wrong with mom?," our son Adriaan asked me. He was on vacation from his boarding school in South Africa and was visiting us. I hadn't noticed anything was amiss with Betsy before he asked. But now I saw it—she was behaving strangely. She was pacing back and forth through the house, seemingly without purpose. She was forgetting everyday words and forgetting to cook meals and couldn't sleep. The compassionate and loving listener was gone. She showed no emotion all. She appeared to be exhausted all the time and seemed totally overwhelmed even when I just mentioned having guests over for coffee. I realized that this had been going on for a few months already.

Thinking about it, I realized that I too had developed some strange behaviors. I sent an email to Rod, our field leader at the time. He called me the moment he got my message. Fortunately, we had phones by then. He asked me a couple of pointed questions: "Is she doing this, is she doing that?" It was as if he'd been watching us. "Compassion fatigue," was his conclusion.

I had never heard of compassion fatigue, but I knew instantly what it meant. We had been giving and giving love and compassion for so long that our emotional batteries had gone flat. There was nothing left. The average life expectancy in Mozambique, at the time, was only forty-nine. That meant we were regularly attending funerals. We were surrounded by extremely poor people who always seemed to be hungry. There was no way we could look after all of them. It was overwhelming.

Missionaries tend to tough it out—we had to. But sometimes we overdid it. The value of a good missions agency is to know when to step in when things get too much. World Outreach does not control people, allowing missionaries to take the initiative. But in certain cases, like ours at the time, the field leader intervened tactfully and lovingly. Rod said, "Get out of there immediately."

Within a week we found ourselves back in South Africa with appointments that Rod had set up for us to see two counselors. Rod also explained matters to our pastor in South Africa, Lourens, and to our supporters. His actions saved our sanity and our ministry. Since this incident, we urge all missionaries to join a good missions agency like World Outreach.

Both counselors agreed. To recuperate, we had to stay out of Mozambique for at least six months. Six months? We were appalled. We can't just leave the Iso for six months! And what would happen to our house? Who will pay the rent and the bills? Yet, there it was. If we wanted to have a long life in ministry, that was the price we had to pay. We had no choice.

One of our supporters offered us their holiday home to use in South Africa. The house had a beautiful view of the ocean. It was peaceful and quiet, not like the constant flow of beggars and sick or dying people in *ParkingTicket*. It was perfect for us to recuperate in, to rest and regroup.

But after two months, Betsy was still in a pretty bad shape not even bothering to change out of her pajamas at all. I was worried. She wasn't snapping out of it. That was, until the Lord intervened in a most unusual way.

In the middle of the night we were woken up by the sound of glass being broken. I switched on the light and stared down the barrel of a sub-machine gun. It was a home invasion. There were three men, screaming and threatening to kill us. By this time we had been threatened by people waving and pointing AK-47's at us in Mozambique, but this was different. I could see murder in the leader's eyes. He was really planning on killing us.

Betsy just stood there like a pillar of salt, motionless, her brain frozen. My insides were shaking. I could only manage to whisper, "Jesus, Jesus, Jesus." A thought flashed through my mind. What would it feel like to get shot? I could see the gun was aimed at my chest. I hoped that it would be quick. A sudden rush of excitement—I'm going to see Jesus within a minute or two. But then came the thought: what would happen to our kids if we died?

One of the robbers went off to collect the loot—computers, cell phones, wallets, anything that looked valuable.

Slowly, I became aware of the fact that the gunman was actually afraid of *me*. He was all show: screaming, pointing the gun around, yet his nervousness and volatility made the situation more precarious. And abruptly, just as quick as they had appeared, they were gone.

Our phones had been stolen so we couldn't contact the police or anybody else. There was a panic button in the house, but the alarm wasn't working. We hid in the bathroom, in case they decided to come back. Once daylight came, we drove to the neighbors who phoned the police.

After the police came over, we had the broken window fixed and decided to leave. We drove back to our home base in another town, staying the rest of the time with our pastor and his wife, who made sure we were pampered and well taken care of.

Where was God in all this? He was right there with us. And just like the Bible is true, God works all things together for the good of those who love Him (Romans 8:28). Three days later, Betsy suddenly "woke up" from her compassion fatigue induced dream-state. I had my wife back. Her normal sharp and clear mind was there, her sense of humor, and hope for the future. God had used that incident like a type of shock treatment, "shocking" her back into the land of the living.

We still had to go for some counseling for PTSD[22] afterward. But two sessions of this fixed us both. In the end, instead of six months, we were cleared to go back to Mozambique in only three months. God had been with us all the way, and He used a violent home invasion to snap us out of it.

While we had been hiding in the bathroom after the robbers had left, we decided to forgive them. We didn't want to be stuck with all kinds of baggage and unforgiveness. After forgiving them, I asked the Lord to remove them from society because I knew they were going to hurt someone. A while after the event, the police informed us that two of the men had

22 Post-traumatic stress disorder

been killed in a shootout with the police, and the other one had been arrested. The Lord still answers David-like prayers. Read Psalm 20.

Stinky demon

Henry, Mozambique

What was that smell? It hit us like a wall—thick, suffocating, impossible to ignore. We were no strangers to bad odors. After all, we lived on a beach that doubled as a toilet. To dig a "long drop," people had to dig a hole and line it with cement, because our village was built on sea sand. The Iso were too poor to build such long drops. So they used the beach instead, as their ancestors had done for centuries. They didn't dig holes—they simply left it on top of the sand and rocks. We lived in a bay, so there were no big waves to wash things away, only gentle lapping water. The "evidence" of last night's dinner stayed on the beach. So did the smell. There is a famous beach in Rio de Janeiro called the Copacabana. We called our beach the *Cocó*cabana—cocó being the Portuguese word for poo.

In addition to this, fishermen used to string up rays that they had caught, leaving them to dry in the sun. These dried rays were like jerky or biltong. The stench of them drying out was overpowering—imagine the smell of rotten fish, multiplied by a hundred.

On a good day, we would have only one smell—the toilet beach or the rays. On a bad day, both. But this day was worse. Much worse. The stench was so overpowering we could hardly breathe. I went outside to see if there were rays drying out. Nothing. This was certainly not normal.

Annoyed, after trying to breathe through this stench for a long time, I blurted out in frustration, "This just isn't natural!" The moment I said it, realization dawned on me. I was right. It wasn't natural at all.

Perhaps we were smelling demons? Could that be?

Right there, we began to pray, rebuking Satan in the name of Jesus. And in an instant, an *instant*, the stench was gone! No breeze, no sudden shift in the wind. Just God, silencing the stench of darkness with His power. See Luke 10:17-19.

Flip-flop of doom

Betsy, Mozambique

Our old Portuguese-style house had one bathroom. Outside, for backup, we had a "long drop." At one point, we had a large family visiting—seven people sharing that one bathroom. Meanwhile, I had malaria. (If you've never had malaria, let me enlighten you: it comes with… urgent, frequent bathroom visits). I nobly ceded the indoor bathroom to our guests and started using the outdoor long drop myself.

I was preparing for, shall we say, "business as usual," when disaster struck. The ground around the cement lid gave way. Suddenly, my leg plunged straight into the toilet hole—up to my knee—dangling in no-man's-land. I managed to pull myself out, scraped and shaken, but okay. However, one of my flip-flops didn't make it. It was gone—sacrificed to the abyss.

Days later, our guard came to me, smiling proudly, holding… my missing flip-flop, all cleaned up and ready to be worn. Don't ask. Please, don't even imagine. Some stories are too traumatic to picture.

Needless to say, I never wore that flip-flop again.

The visitors and the chickens

Betsy, Mozambique

For weeks we were buzzing with excitement. A small group of friends and supporters from South Africa were coming to visit us for the very first time. They had never set foot among the Iso, and we couldn't wait to show them our world—our friends, our life, the good, the bad, and yes... the downright ugly.

Now, we lived *very* simply. Our house sat on the edge of *ParkingTicket*. It had cement floors full of cracks and potholes, a roof that was half cement, half corrugated iron, depending on what scraps were available. Mosquito nets hung like drapery everywhere. Our front room didn't even have glass windows, just mosquito netting—so whenever the rains came, we had to sprint to rescue anything that was not waterproof.

Electricity? Occasionally. Water? Sometimes. And our toilet? Well... we technically lived on a toilet beach. Yes, the village beach doubled as the community restroom. But luckily, we had a toilet in our house and a "long drop" outside. Let's just say it was hot, humid, and not exactly smelling of roses.

Still, this was our normal. I knew our supporters would be kind, but I also worried about how they'd see our "rustic" lifestyle. So, I scrubbed, tidied, and did everything I could to make things look presentable. I was determined that, for one shining weekend, our little home would look less like survival mode and more like missionary chic.

And then—the chickens ruined it.

When the kids were still living with us, they found a stray cat, which they promptly named "Elvis." We'd cut a little flap in the front mosquito net as a door for her to come and go. Lovely idea for the cat. Unfortunately, the chickens figured it out too.

And so there we were, sitting with our guests in the living room, drinking instant coffee and telling stories, when suddenly—in strutted a few chickens, bold as brass, pecking their way across the living room floor like they owned the place. Everybody laughed—me too, but it probably sounded more like a hysterical giggle.

I nearly died of embarrassment. However, I put on my most stern voice and shooed them out as quickly as possible.

For years, just thinking about that moment made me cringe. Until, one day, I mentioned it to my friend who had been there that day. She looked at me blankly and said she couldn't even remember it. Out of courtesy? Selective memory? Or maybe God Himself, in His mercy, deleted the experience from her mind.

Either way, I finally made peace with it. Lesson learned: die to yourself, laugh, be real. After all… they're only chickens.

Another "Mama" story

Henry, Mozambique

We were once sitting outside *Mama's* house, together with her extended family. *Mama* was the woman who had decided that she was our Iso mother. The day before, a powerful gust of wind had blown across the bay and swept through our little village. In seconds, it brought down bamboo fences and uprooted tall palm trees, including one at our house.

I asked *Mama* if this happened often. She replied, "No, only when the dragon across the bay burps." Of course I cracked up laughing—until I saw she was completely serious. I instantly swallowed my laughter with a gulp. If I hadn't, she'd never again confide any of her thoughts with us. And if you want to share the gospel clearly and effectively, you need to know the deepest beliefs of the people. Well, this was what *Mama* and her family believed.

The little dog God used to save us—twice

Henry, Mozambique

Lizette, our friend from the orphanage, was moving to Maputo in the south of Mozambique and asked us to take her cheeky little Jack Russell dog, Rocky, along on our four-and-a-half-day drive to South Africa. I wasn't sure how that would work out—fourteen hours a day in the car with a little dog, for four days? But the kids were thrilled. Rocky turned out to be a star traveler. He loved all the attention he got while they were teaching him all kinds of tricks. His best one? At the command: "Speed cop," (Afrikaans slang for a traffic policeman), he would curl back his lips and growl ferociously. Funny.

Two days later, we had to cross the mile-wide Zambezi River on a "ferry"—planks tied together and mounted on oil drums, diesel engines smoking, with no railings, and plenty of thieves around. As we crossed the river, an Iso truck driver with a large poster of Osama bin Laden in his truck, warned us about corrupt police on the other side who rob people who travel through at night. He advised us to sleep over on the other side of the river. But that place across the river was a dump, known to be infested with mosquitoes and thieves. We reluctantly decided to drive on.

Darkness descended while we were driving along this isolated dirt road. Then sure enough, there they were: two officers armed with AK-47s. They waved us down. My heart pounded as one swaggered toward us arrogantly, holding an AK-47 in his hands. I knew this was trouble.

"Open the window," the kids whispered. The moment the policeman got to the car, they softly said to Rocky, "Speed cop." Rocky let out a vicious snarl, lips curled back, growling like ferocious wild animal. The officer froze, then barked out (that's a pun) one word, "Go!" We drove off immediately, quite stunned by what just happened. We knew Rocky had saved us from what could have been a nightmare.

Hours of driving later, we still had not found a safe place to stay over. We were exhausted. Near a crossroads was a dingy, grimy truck stop. As our grandkids, Monét and Jude, would say, it looked really "suss"—suspicious. But we felt we had no choice but to stay there overnight.

There was a drinking tavern with rowdy drunks, and next to it, a few small flimsy rooms in a row with very flimsy-looking doors. The doors had no latches, never mind locks. A lot of trucks were parked outside. We had to get two rooms. One was too small for all of us. My dilemma was, do I put Betsy and Esté in one room with Adriaan and me in the other, or do we put the kids together in a room. We could see people watching us carefully. I decided to put the kids and Rocky in one room, and Betsy and I in the other. We told them to barricade themselves by stacking suitcases against the door. We did the same, knowing that even the slightest push would open the door.

None of us slept much. Around four a.m., Rocky erupted into action, growling furiously and barking ferociously. Someone had started opening the door of their room, moving the suitcases. But apparently, they had second thoughts after hearing, what sounded to them, like a viscious monster dog inside.

They would have been ashamed to know that a cute, sweet little lap dog had scared them away. On one day, God had used a little dog to save us from harm—twice. Who said angels have to be big, imposing shiny figures with white robes and wings?

CHAPTER TEN

MARCHING ORDERS

---CRXO---

"Go to Asia to train missionaries"

Henry, Mozambique

After about seven years in Mozambique, I got the impression that God said, "Go to Asia and train missionaries." What? A hundred questions flooded my mind. Training missionaries? Who would want me to train them? And where in Asia? We were not done with our work among the Iso. What about the flowers in the desert? There was still much work to be done.

All these questions were running through my head. Had I heard wrong? I told Betsy about it. "No, you heard wrong," she flatly stated. I've always trusted her discernment, yet I was *sure* that I had heard God correctly, even though I didn't yet know what this new direction would look like.

We started praying. Seriously. One of my concerns was that maybe I subconsciously just wanted a way out. Life in *ParkingTicket* was hard. Was this "call" I heard just an excuse to get out of there? Yet the more I prayed, the more I felt convinced that God was telling us to move. I had the feeling that the move would happen in about three years' time. But Betsy still felt unsure about moving.

So, like Gideon of old, we put out a "fleece" (Judges 6:36-40). In fact, we put out two. In the seven years we had lived there, we had never been able to find people willing to join our little team of two. And this was not for a lack of trying, praying and asking. We began asking God to send us people to take over from us, then we would leave. This was the first "fleece." The second was that He would open doors for us in missions training.

We both knew that both requests were impossible for us to engineer. For example, we felt it would be highly unlikely for people to come and carry on the work we had started in a period of only three years. Such people would have to raise support, relocate to Mozambique, learn Portuguese, and at least start learning Isoni before we left. And training? Where would we find people in Asia to train? We hardly knew anyone there.

Yet God started answering our prayers rapidly. Within a few weeks the *God-incidents* started happening. First, our missions agency contacted us. "Would you consider joining our new training team?," they asked. Duh. Yes!

Then, *God-incidentally*, another missions agency held a retreat for their missionaries in the town nearby and invited us to join them for a meal. They asked us to share about our approach to the work among the Iso. The next day one of the missionary couples, T and M[23], came to our house to talk with us some more.

And this is where God's faithfulness kicked into high gear. This couple wanted to move to Isoland and join us. They

23   Names withheld for security reasons.

were seasoned missionaries, having been in Mozambique for much longer than we had. They had already raised the financial support they needed. They spoke Portuguese. And they were eager to learn Isoni. A week or so later T phoned me and what he said stunned me, "I want you to train us." Us? Train *them*?

God's timing was perfect. After a year or so, they were there with us in Isoland. This gave them plenty of time for orientation, transition and Isoni language study well before we left. Isn't God just the best? His timing is perfect. He answers audacious and even cheeky prayers because of His graciousness and loving devotion.

For us, things started speeding up. Our missions agency sent us to Sydney, Australia, to learn how to be missionary trainers. And it was there, in the middle of a training session, that Betsy finally accepted our future. She was now ready to leave the Iso.

We served for many years on World Outreach's course development team. I was also invited to join the senior International Leadership Team—a role that required me to travel to Singapore twice a year. I accepted the position two years before our relocation to Asia, which gave me the opportunity to become familiar with that part of the world.

The new chapter in our journey had arrived wondrously. Our faithful God had made the way unmistakably clear. But it always remained a journey of faith. For now, however, we were still in Mozambique.

The tsunami that tested my priorities

Henry, Mozambique

Have you ever had cause to stop and consider your priorities in life in a very real way? Well, this happened to us once. The Iso often sent us "beepies"—they would call us on the cell phone (yes, even some of the Iso had those later on), but would hang up before we could answer. They couldn't afford to make the call, so we had to call them back. How could such poor people afford cell phones, you ask? Well, there seemed to have been an almost endless supply of cheap, second-hand phones from South Africa making their way there. But I digress.

There we were, minding our own business one evening, when we got a "beepy." Maybe a sick person had to go to the clinic? Betsy called back, and the woman said that it had been announced on the radio that people close to shore had to evacuate their houses. Now you should realize that all kinds of "interesting stories" abounded there. You'll remember *Mama*'s story about the dragon that burped.

We were skeptical about this news. But then another "beepy" came in from someone else. This time with more details. There had been an enormous earthquake under the sea near Indonesia and a tsunami was on the way. Everyone living within 150 yards of the shore had to evacuate their houses within thirty minutes. *Now* they had our attention. Our house was right on the beach. Because of a previous tsunami—a "sudden high tide" to the north of us—had seven people drowned. It could happen again.

Our house was about ten meters from, and about 1.5 meters above, the high-tide mark. So now we faced the dilemma of having to decide very quickly which of our "earthly treasures" were important enough for us to pack and take with us, and which ones we could leave behind. Remember, we had no insurance.

Surprisingly, when it came down to it, the decision wasn't so difficult. This was, in fact, a pleasant surprise to us. Our kids didn't live there anymore, so we needn't worry about them. Obviously, we had to leave. With some basic clothes and medicine. The next priority was our passports and the cash we had in the house. After that came the computers and recording equipment, which contained almost a year's work. Then we were away to high ground.

At about ten p.m. that night, the "all clear" was sounded, but we stayed overnight with our friends at the Leprosy Mission in town anyway. We felt a bit like fools—but hey, some excitement was welcome.

The next morning, as we were driving back home, we saw what looked like a scene out of a movie. "Refugees" were carrying suitcases and small kids on their backs, all returning home. For some of our Iso friends, leaving their homes had been an even more difficult decision to make. They knew that if they left their mud huts, their possessions would probably be stolen. So many of them decided to stay, not knowing what was going to happen.

In retrospect, it was a privilege to be confronted with a situation where we had to decide quickly what was *really* important to us, and what was not. It prepared us for our move to Southeast Asia, because not long after this incident, we relocated with two suitcases, two laptop bags and our trust in God.

"Do not store up for yourselves treasures on earth, where moth and rust destroy, and where thieves break in and steal. But store up for yourselves treasures in heaven, where moth and rust do not destroy, and where thieves do not break in and steal. For where your treasure is, there your heart will be also" (Matthew 6:19-21).

The Nations Course

Henry, Africa, Asia, Australasia

An old, dignified pastor once stood before a group of missionaries at an orientation event in Kenya. Gravely, he said the following:

"We truly appreciate that you have come to our country with such passion for the lost. You gave up everything to live and minister here. We understand that you will make cultural mistakes. But please, make *new* mistakes. Don't make the same mistakes your predecessors made."

His statement reminds me of the following sayings: "Those who cannot remember the past are condemned to repeat it,"[24] and, "The only thing we learn from history is that we learn nothing from history."[25]

This idea has shaped the way Betsy and I train new missionaries. We tell them early on in our courses, "We've made many mistakes. We'll share these with you freely. Then you'll be able to go and make your own new and original mistakes. Just don't repeat ours." We enjoyed teaching World Outreach's Nations Course because for us it was not just theory learned from books. We had personal experience of most of what we taught. And that carried weight.

24 Santayana, a Spanish philosopher.
25 Hegel, a German philosopher and theologian.

We taught this course to new and experienced missionaries in many places, including South Africa, Kenya, Malaysia, Thailand, and New Zealand. We were course leaders in South Africa and Kenya.

Surprisingly, not everyone arrived eager to learn. Some seasoned missionaries were reluctant to step away from their ministries for six weeks to attend the course. Some were gently encouraged, or "required," to take the course by their leaders. I remember one such experienced missionary. During the first week, his body language shouted out: "I don't want to be here!" His arms were folded tightly, and he had a thinly disguised scowl on his face. I knew this man, and such behavior was totally unlike him.

But not long after we started teaching, something in his demeanor shifted. He leaned forward, listening intently. He began to look less like someone forced to endure a family reunion. By the second week, he was the most vocal in the class—asking questions, debating points, and filling pages with notes. He discovered what every missionary eventually must, and that is that no one knows everything. We should all keep on learning. After the course we read in his newsletters about how his ministry had improved remarkably as he adopted some of what he had learned.

Another time, we had a large, diverse group—over thirty students, with ages ranging from nineteen to fifty-five. One day, the youngest, a bright-eyed nineteen-year-old girl, sat beside the oldest student, a veteran who had been on the field for as long as she had been alive. As I was speaking, and in response to a statement I made, she blurted out, "That just can't be true!" The older man turned to her and gently but convincingly said, "That is *exactly* how it is." Then he shared a story from his own ministry. In that moment, the truth of my statement had more weight because it was confirmed by a peer's hard-won experience.

Betsy, Kenya

At another time, we were teaching the course in Kenya. Most of the students were Kenyans, mostly college graduates. As part of the course, I taught a class on orality— understanding how people who can't, or prefer not to read, learn new things. They prefer to learn by listening to stories, concrete stories about people and relationships. About 70% of the world's population is like this. They are called "Concrete-relational learners." I taught these highly literate, college-educated Kenyans how to share Bible stories in ways that oral people would remember, retell, and apply to their lives.

Afterward, their mission leader came to me with a grave face. "I mourn for lost opportunities," he said. His words startled me. Then he explained that for years he had sent his teams to largely illiterate villages where they tried to present the gospel in an academic and logical way—a way that meant little to oral learners. They had limited success. The opportunities had slipped away. When he learned about this approach, he realized that this was how they should have done evangelism from the beginning.

To his credit, he did something about his regret. He embraced these new concepts, and soon the entire group was confidently telling Bible stories in a way that their listeners could truly grasp.

Caught with my pants down

Betsy, Mozambique

Driving in Mozambique was never boring. It was either an adventure or a nightmare, depending on how much the suspension of your vehicle—or your spine—could handle. The "roads" ranged from pothole obstacle courses to "choose-your-own-adventure" paths where you just sort of guessed where the road should be. Spoiler alert: sometimes there wasn't one.

Don't even begin to think about pit stops or convenience stores. No gas stations, no restrooms, no drive-thru cappuccinos—just endless bush, mud huts dotted along the road, and the occasional landmine warning sign to spice things up.

So, what did we do when nature called? Easy. We had the system down pat: Men went behind the bushes on one side of the road; women took the bushes on the other side. Efficient. Uncomplicated. Until it wasn't.

One time, while escorting our field leaders on a trip, the inevitable moment came. Off we went—men to one side, my friend and I to the other. I gave her a little demonstration on the fine art of "bush etiquette"—how to squat just right—when suddenly, out of nowhere, a massive truck barreled past. Dust flying, engine roaring, the load bed packed full of people. Not just any people—*my* people, the people from *ParkingTicket*.

And there I was, head poking above the bushes, mid-squat. The truck erupted in cheers. "*Nu Beti*!!!" (Older Sister Betsy), they shouted, waving like I was in a parade. Except, you know… not the kind of parade you ideally want to be in.

I gave the weakest little smile and waved back, face on fire, while Henry and his buddy on the men's side nearly died laughing. By the time we rolled back into *ParkingTicket*, the whole place knew exactly what I was doing, where I was doing it, and with whom. It seemed that in Africa, news traveled faster than diarrhea.

Snake story

Henry, Mozambique

We often jokingly remark that most missionaries seem to collect toilet- and snake stories, especially in Africa, the way tourists collect fridge magnets. I must confess that I am very afraid of snakes. On that note, here's my snake story.

As the time for our departure from Mozambique was drawing near, Betsy and I visited the World Outreach colleagues living in Mozambique to say goodbye. One couple was away at the time, so we stayed at their house. We were accompanied by Rod and Lynley, our African Directors at the time. The house was small, with space for only two to sleep inside. The house had a flat roof with a structure made of bamboo on top, like a kind of open-air rooftop veranda. We would sleep there in a little tent that night, and Rod and Lynley took the room inside.

The afternoon was swelteringly hot. Betsy and I went up to the roof for a siesta. Because it was so hot, I stretched out on a mattress, shirtless, and soon drifted off to sleep.

My nap didn't last long. I was jolted awake by what felt like a whip lightly lashing across my back. I sat up, and there —staring right into my eyes—was a green mamba. Yes, *the* green mamba, one of Africa's deadliest snakes. My heart didn't just skip a beat—it filed for early retirement. Abruptly, I found myself standing on the other side of the roof, almost as if I'd been teleported right across the roof. In that moment, I forgot everything, even to pray.

Apparently, the snake had been slithering along the bamboo rafters, minding its own business, when it suddenly saw this white man lying below it. The shock of this unexpected sight must have caused it to lose its footing (can snakes even have a footing?), resulting in its fall, right on top of my back. If I was terrified, I can only assume the snake was equally so—because by the time I had teleported, it was gone.

Needless to say, Betsy and I evacuated that roof faster than you can say "snake." There was no way were we were going to sleep on that roof that night, so we made ourselves a bed on the floor at Rod and Lynley's feet. A very cozy arrangement.

Later, colleagues who lived nearby cheerfully told us they knew about the snake. "What, and you didn't tell me?," I asked, rather taken aback. They replied that it wasn't really a green mamba, but some harmless impostor that just happens to look exactly like one. Well, almost exactly. It's easy to tell the difference, they said. The color of the inside of a mamba's mouth is more of a dark bluish color, and that of that fake mamba snake was more purplish. Well, thank you so very much for enlightening me. There was no way I was going to linger around and kindly request any snake to open its mouth so I could see what color its gums were. For me, snake equals snake equals snake.

Spared from evil

Betsy, Mozambique

There is a moment that is forever burned into my memory. Friday, 6pm. July 9th, 2010.

We had one week left before our scheduled flight back to South Africa. We were preparing to relocate from Mozambique to Southeast Asia. Just as we were sitting down to have a farewell meal with friends, my phone rang. Calls from unknown numbers are so annoying. I answered anyway. In that moment, I heard the most devastating words ever spoken to me. Time froze. "I am so sorry to tell you that your son has just died." I called out to Henry, but no sound came out of my mouth. I was not breathing. I had just died too.

What followed was a blur. We contacted friends in South Africa for help, even though we were not able to think clearly. This just couldn't be true. It was urgent to contact our daughter in America and tell her, otherwise she might read about this on social media before we had informed her. Only God could give such presence of mind, and courage to be able to phone her in that moment. How do you tell your pregnant daughter that her beloved brother of nineteen has just died?

You just do.

I had no tears. It worried me. Why was I not crying? Henry's eyes scared me—pools of unspeakable pain and grief. No words were spoken between us. We just kept on looking at each other, helplessly.

We were scheduled to fly to South Africa in exactly nine days. "God, what is this with Your timing?," I thought. "Couldn't we just have seen him one last time?"

Henry

It felt as if some wild animal had pushed its claws right into my chest and torn it open. That night I cried out to God, "Jesus promised to send us the Comforter, so where is He now?" Instantly I saw a vision of Adriaan. He was wearing the fanciest tuxedo, complete with frilly shirt and white shoes. He struck a pose as if saying, "Look at me, who's the man?" He always liked to dress nicely and to strike up hilarious poses. But never had I seen him dressed so smartly. That second, I knew he was okay. He was with Jesus. It gave me a measure of peace. But the pain in my heart was unbearable.

Betsy

When they heard about Adriaan, our Iso friends came over to mourn with us. They were well-trained in mourning—most of the women had lost at least one child. This was not sympathy, but empathy. The women just sat with me; no words were needed.

Then we flew back to South Africa. I couldn't eat, couldn't sleep, wouldn't think. Why was I swallowing all the time? This couldn't be true.

Adriaan didn't have a last will and testament, and this was a legal problem. What kid at age nineteen has a will anyway? For a short while I was mad at him for causing us so much trouble. What had happened? I thought he was healthy. The doctors at the clinic who tried to revive him explained that he had had a brain aneurysm. Dead the instant he fell to the floor in the mall. So, I should be happy he did not suffer? We never got confirmation of this because the government lost the autopsy report.

He loved Jesus. Like Enoch, he "walked faithfully with God, and then he was no more, because God had taken him away" (Genesis 5:24). "He is in a better place now," people assured us. I didn't *want* him to be in a better place. I wanted him to be with *me*. I wanted to celebrate his birthdays, see him fall in love, and babysit his children.

Still not eating, not sleeping, only thinking. No tears.

I couldn't be angry at anyone. He wasn't murdered, he didn't have bad friends who made him do stupid things, he didn't do drugs, nothing. So, it was no-one's fault. This was good, right? Frustrated at not being able to vent my anger, I took it out on God. I was mad because He didn't tell me why. Best friends tell one another everything, right?

"Are you going to leave Me now?," I heard Him softly speaking in my spirit.

Where would I go, Lord? *You* have the words of eternal life. It is still "yes," it will always be "yes."

Here is a quiz: Children whose parents die are called orphans. Someone who loses their spouse is called a widow or widower. What then do you call parents who lose a child? Devastated. You become part of a club no-one wants to belong to.

It's like this—you have an accident and your leg is amputated. It's very painful and traumatic. You almost die from shock. You are sick, you can't do anything. Then the wound heals slowly. It's tender to the touch though. You must re-adjust and do things differently. After some time, you get fitted with a prosthetic leg, and you learn to walk again. Eventually, if you walk down the street wearing trousers, no-one will know that you have only one leg. But *you* know. You always will. You can never grow another leg.

Who do you invite to your nineteen-year-old son's funeral? What songs should be sung? Really? No parent should make decisions like these. But you do. God is there, comforting you, carrying you, crying with you, long-distance through His faithful ones, the Jesus-loving friends who awkwardly want to help, but don't know how. They are the ones who drive you around, bring you food and papers to sign, and help you to choose a casket. The ones who cry so much, you must comfort them. The ones who drink coffee with you without tasting it, looking like their child had died too.

Our daughter was in her last trimester of pregnancy and couldn't fly to South Africa for the funeral. Now she had to help us decide whether to bury or cremate her beloved brother —over the phone. This is unfair. And we can't even hug.

Great funeral—it should be illegal to say this. We decided to let everyone write messages on his casket. It was good for his friends to do this. Bizarre. Yet liberating. I don't know why.

It was a Sunday, two days after the funeral. We had nothing to do, except grieve, so we went to church. That was a waste of time—didn't hear a thing. I had left my brain at home so that I didn't have to think.

A woman came up to us after the service, offering her condolences. Said she knew *exactly* what we were going through. No, please! I didn't have the capacity to hear someone else's tragedy. Apparently, they had a hamster that had died two weeks before. They were all still devastated. So she knew exactly what were going through, she said. She elaborated by saying that when the kids came home from school, they saw the empty cage and cried again. She would try to console them again. She assured us, yet again, that she knew exactly what we were going through. We told her we were so very sorry about their hamster that had died. Was he in a better place too? We could only manage to slowly walk back to the car. No words.

In the privacy of the car, Henry and I gave each other a long look, still no words. Then, as if on cue, we both exploded into laughter. Really? Adriaan would have laughed his head off about the dead hamster. That was his kind of humor. We had to phone Esté and tell her. More hysterical laughter from all of us. She succinctly summed up the situation. If it were a racehorse, or maybe a pedigree dog that had died, it would do justice, but a "blooming rat?" More hysterical laughter. Oh, it feels so good to laugh again.

And finally, the tears came.

Postscript: God eventually *did* tell us why He allowed our beloved son to be taken away in the blink of an eye. He told us in His perfect timing, when He knew we could think clearly again, and would appreciate His awesome, good and perfect will. He took us to this verse:

"The righteous perish, and no one takes it to heart; the devout are taken away, and no one understands that the righteous are taken away to be spared from evil" (Isaiah 57:1).

After many years of practice, I have adapted to walk quite well with this "prosthetic leg." Sometimes I still have this fleeting thought, "It didn't really happen, did it?" Often, I just don't want to remember, because it makes me too sad. On the other hand, I *want* to remember, because I worry that I will forget him—the sound of his voice, the way he smiled for photos with his eyes closed, the way he laughed. People tell me to think of all the good memories we have of him. That's supposed to make me happy.

I have learned that "hope" is not a vague, futile concept, like hoping you will not gain weight if you eat a whole jar of peanut butter. Hope has become an absolute certainty about Jesus' amazing promises. I am not hoping that I will see my son in heaven one day. I *know* I will. I just have to wait.

The earthquake and the broken tooth

Henry, New Zealand

We were in the process of transitioning to Southeast Asia. It was a few months after Adriaan had died when we went to Christchurch in New Zealand for six weeks to teach the Nations Course. We were so relieved that we could be in a safe and friendly place. We were still in shock after Adriaan's death, tired easily and were emotionally very fragile.

The day after the course finished, we went to a mall. I went into a book shop, and Betsy to a little curio shop next door. We had two more days before our flight out.

I always knew that New Zealand was like a large ship on the open ocean, and without warning, this was confirmed—we hit stormy seas. At first, it sounded like a derailed train was coming straight through the shopping mall. The ground started shaking severely as a massive 6.3 earthquake struck. The epicenter was near the surface, only five kilometers (three miles) underground. It was bad.

Trying to keep my balance, I looked in shock as the bookshelves started "walking" toward me. We heard afterward that people were killed in another bookstore when a shelf fell on them. Trying to stand during the shock waves felt like being in a small boat on a very choppy sea. I moved quickly, but unsteadily, to go to stand in the doorway, where it was safer. People were screaming. The cement floor of this enclosed mall was making waves—like waves on the ocean. I couldn't believe my eyes.

Then the power went off. In the dark, I used my phone as a flashlight and made my way to the shop where Betsy was, navigating the "waves," and calling out her name. She replied, and I made my way to her over all kinds of goods that had fallen to the ground. She was lying flat on the floor, dazed. I helped her up, and we moved quickly to the mall's exit, where people were milling about, shock and disbelief on their faces.

There was a dear old lady who was shaking from shock. We tried to console her, but just as she had calmed down, an aftershock hit. Everything started shaking again. We offered to drive her to her granddaughter's house nearby. Betsy drove her car, and I followed in our borrowed car. Luckily, she could remember where her granddaughter lived.

As we were waiting to get into the traffic, another huge aftershock hit. This time it was a 5.7 on the Richter scale. The cars were swaying and swerving as if pranksters were jumping on them, bouncing them. We saw a concrete lamp post swinging back and forth, like a pendulum. I estimated it swayed at about a thirty-degree angle from side to side. This was a most uncomfortable sight to see. We heard afterward that elsewhere in the city such a pole had snapped and cut a car in half.

Another motorist told me afterwards how he had been driving along the motorway, when the earthquake hit, causing cars to swerve violently all over the road. As we drove, I could see that the normally safe, predictable drivers were in a panic. All the traffic lights were out, too. It was chaos.

After we dropped the lady off at her daughter's home, we realized that we had no idea where we were. We didn't know the city, and there was no GPS in the car. We pulled off the road and waited somewhere for the traffic to die down while asking God to get us home.

While driving back, hoping we were going in the right direction, we saw schoolchildren walking along the road, crying. The streets had large cracks in them. Emergency vehicles were screaming past. Betsy only then discovered that when she fell, she had broken off one of her teeth.

We got back to the house at last and found that our host's house was fine, but with all kinds of items strewn over the floors. Betsy went to the bathroom to relieve some stress and was still there when another aftershock hit. It's not a good place to be, on the swaying top floor of a two-story story house. Let me just say she had to make some very rapid decisions.

The electricity and the Internet were still working in that part of the city. We saw that Esté, in America, was on Skype, so we called her. We didn't want her to hear about the earthquake from somewhere else and worry about us. We switched on the video so we could see one another. We had just told Esté and her husband Matt what was going on, when another powerful aftershock hit. We had moved the computer close to the sliding door of the veranda, so we both fled outside. While everything was still quaking, I realized that they must have gotten a huge fright when we abruptly disappeared, so I quickly ran inside, told them we were okay, and shot outside again.

Once the shaking stopped, we went back inside again. And there were these two shocked faces on the computer screen. I got the giggles—maybe it was delayed hysterics—from seeing the expression on their faces. They had just seen us running out of the screen's view, saw everything shaking and swaying in the house, things falling over, items breaking... I think that one had been a 5.4 aftershock. A powerful earthquake in its own right.

The tower of the old Canterbury Cathedral, an iconic and beautiful building in Christchurch, had collapsed. People were trapped in there for a long time. We had just been there a week before. Elsewhere in the city, a four-story building collapsed completely, pancaking on top of itself, trapping and crushing people. In other places, people were trapped under their desks at work. A huge boulder rolled down a hill in a town nearby and destroyed a building. Fires started due to gas leaks. Two buses full of people were crushed by falling buildings. "There but for the grace of God go we!"

We saw some liquefaction along the road. I had never heard of "liquefaction" before this event. Wikipedia defines it as follows: "Soil liquefaction describes a phenomenon whereby a soil substantially loses strength and stiffness in response to an applied stress, usually earthquake shaking or other rapid loading (force), causing it to behave like a liquid."

On television, they showed a sizable patch of soil churning into a whirlpool. One woman, rushing out of her house as the earthquake struck, sank down to her knees in her lawn. Weird.

We spent one night sleeping on the ground floor, crammed in with others who had come seeking safety at the house we were staying in. Our flight was scheduled for the next day, but the airport had shut down while engineers inspected the runways for cracks. By God's grace, we managed to board when it reopened. As the plane lifted off, the cabin erupted in cheers. No more earthquakes, Lord—please!

Looking back at that time, we realized that over an eight-month period we had lost our son, left Mozambique and our friends after ten years, experienced an earthquake, hid in the basement of our daughter's house twice because of two tornadoes passing nearby, witnessed the birth of our first grandchild, Monét, born prematurely, and relocated to a new country in Southeast Asia. But our faithful God was with us every step of the way.

The Lord took us not only to a new country, but to a new vision. He told us He would lead us into a season of rest and renewal, even though our days were occupied with work. He told us that He would put us under a big tree for our provision and for our protection. And He did. Sometime later, we found out that the name of the town we had moved to in Southeast Asia was named after a big, shady tree. And so it was.

CHAPTER ELEVEN

NOODLES AND NOMADS

———⟨⟩———

A new vision

Henry and Betsy, New Zealand

While we were still in New Zealand, after the earthquake and just before our move to Southeast Asia, we prayed and brainstormed together. We knew God had called us to train missionaries in Asia, but we wanted a clear, concise way to explain our goals to others. The answer came almost immediately. We felt God was calling us to "*prepare more effective Kingdom workers.*" More effective, and more of them. And this is what we've been doing ever since.

Almost streetwise

Henry, Southeast Asia

We were in Southeast Asia for a few weeks, training new missionaries for our missions agency. This was before we moved there permanently. To get around the bustling city, I decided to rent a motorbike.

When I was young and restless, I had a motorbike, which made me rather confident about our little adventure. But, this little motorbike almost caused a divorce. Betsy had never ridden a motorbike before. I gave her some tips, but when I got to the part of "leaning into" the corners, she became like a rebellious teenager. She was adamant that we would fall over if we were to do that. I was confused—she was a clever, sharp woman, but the gravity thing was too much for her.

Every time we approached a corner, she instinctively tried to remain upright instead of leaning into the turn. This reaction made the motorbike unstable and caused it to wobble as we navigated around bends. Each trip through the city streets became a true adventure, testing both our patience and our balance. Furthermore, to aggravate everything, I could hear her praying fervently behind me.

We didn't have GPS. It was up to us to figure out how to navigate our way through the maze of streets in heavy traffic and unfamiliar surroundings. We quickly learned that the word for "road" is "jalan." A road near where we stayed was marked "Jalan Sehala" i.e. "Sehala Road." Or so we thought....

We came to the conclusion that *Jalan Sehala* must be a very long road, because right on the other side of the city there was another *Jalan Sehala*. "Strange," I thought, "I could have sworn it ran north-south and not east-west." Shortly after that we found another *Jalan Sehala* in a completely different part of the city. Mr. Sehala must have been a very important person to have so many streets named after him.

Only later did we find out that "Sehala" means "one-way"—all those *Jalan Sehalas* were actually one-way streets! Oops.

Walking by faith

Betsy, Southeast Asia

The traffic in Southeast Asia was… let's say "interesting." No, who am I kidding? It was challenging. Actually—wild. Okay fine, it was a nightmare.

Driving was one thing. At least in a car you had metal around you, and on a motorbike you had… well… speed? But crossing the road on foot? That was an entirely different level of danger.

There were cars bumper to bumper, scooters going the wrong way, carts with heaps of produce, and hundreds of small motorbikes carrying entire families—none of them wearing helmets. We even saw some cows in the road on a few occasions and once a monitor lizard. I would stand on the curb frozen, praying for a gap in traffic that never came. Meanwhile Henry would already be on the other side looking like he just won the American Ninja Warrior context.

Often he would have to come back through the motorized stampede to retrieve me. Eventually, we developed a system: I would clamp onto his arm as if my life depended on it—which, honestly, it might have, stare straight ahead, and wait for his command. His instructions were clear, "When I say 'Go', you go!" On cue, I just walked, eyes glued to the road in front of me and tightly clutching his arm—no looking left, no looking right, no looking at the smoking truck barreling toward us. Just pure, unblinking commitment.

That, my friends, is what I call walking by faith.

Food called SOS

Betsy, Southeast Asia

We loved living in Southeast Asia. One of its greatest charms is the incredible food—abundant, delicious, and wonderfully affordable. But, of course, the world isn't perfect. Enter the noodle challenge. Imagine standing in a supermarket aisle, surrounded by nothing but noodles—aisles and aisles of them, stretching endlessly in every direction. Every shape, every color, every thickness you can imagine. Noodles as far as the eye can see. Which one do you choose? What makes it even more difficult is that most of the labels look like hieroglyphics to you. So, like any clever foreigner, you try a few—and then cling to your favorite brand for dear life.

Finding your favorite tomato sauce was the same ordeal. After some trial and error, we finally found one we liked. The label proudly declared: "SOS." Strange, we thought. Why name a food product after an international distress signal? "Tomato emergency?" "Rescue me with ketchup?" Nevertheless, we decided to be loyal to this brand. SOS it would be.

But, with the next trip to the grocery store, confusion kicked into high gear. Every single tomato sauce bottle was marked SOS. Had the entire tomato industry suddenly gone into crisis? Nope. It turns out that SOS was just the local spelling for the English word "sauce."

At that point, the other shoppers had to be wondering why two foreigners were doubled over in the middle of the store, laughing like two maniacs at the ketchup shelf.

The dreaded "small room"

Henry, Southeast Asia

Every time we had to go through a border checkpoint in Africa and Asia—and trust me, there were many—it was like preparing for a final exam that you hadn't study for. You had to be strategic about it.

Rule number one: Be friendly, but not *too* friendly. No jokes, no sarcasm. Just answer the questions and remain calm.

Rule number two: Don't volunteer information. Ever. If they ask what's in your bag, you don't say, "Snacks and maybe a body." You say, "Clothes."

Rule number three: Look relaxed, but not so relaxed that you seem suspicious. Confident, but not arrogant. Basically, you're supposed to look like James Bond on holiday—minus the gadgets. Or the charm.

In Southeast Asia, we noticed a pattern. The men at the immigration booths were usually somewhat laid-back. They looked at your passport like saying, "Hey, tomorrow is another day." But the women? Oh no. The women were border-control terminators with their no-nonsense, black-and-white approach. They inspected your passport the way a jeweler would inspect diamonds. Every page was scrutinized. Every stamp checked. Probably the glue under the photo, too. And they took their time. They made you sweat.

So naturally, we always tried to line up with a male official. But of course, you don't always get to choose which booth to go to at immigration.

One time, we were traveling by bus from one country to another. The whole busload of passengers got dumped at the one side of the border to walk through customs and immigration. You take everything with you—all your luggage included. When you are through immigration and customs and on the other side of the border, the bus is there waiting for all its passengers to board again. You load your luggage onto the bus again and the trip continues.

Unfortunately, that time we landed in front of a female official. At least we were together. To this day, we don't know what set her off. Maybe I was too friendly. Maybe we just looked like international criminals. Quite suddenly, we were marched off to "The Small Room" by a policeman with a gun. You know, "that room." Every border crossing has one. Nobody wants to go there. It's where dreams go to die.

We sat there forever, marinating in our own sweat, praying, praying... Eventually, a man came in, asked us a bunch of obvious questions. He eventually decided we weren't international criminals and escorted us back to the booth to get our stamps. Victory!

Except... our bus had already left. Yes. The driver had zero interest in waiting for the suspicious couple who were being interrogated and were holding up everybody on the bus. And so there we were, stranded at the border post. It's hot. It's humid. With a heap of luggage. More prayer. It is interesting what kind of prayers you can come up with in situations like these.

Thankfully, another bus eventually rolled by, picked us up, and off we went. Of course, we had to buy new tickets. We always pray when we go through customs and immigration, but after that adventure, we started praying very specifically.

We would pray and ask God to show us where He was in that immigration hall. We knew He was there, but we asked that He give us a picture we could hold onto. And one time afterward, after praying, Betsy had this vision—Jesus, standing with His feet planted on top of the row of booths, towering over the officials. Awesome. Majestic. Unshakable.

Because really—who's in charge after all? Not the lady who holds the stamp.

The tooth and the super glue

Henry, Mozambique, Southeast Asia

It sounds a bit like the title of a modern fable, doesn't it? I'll let you into a deep and dark secret... one of my front teeth is a false tooth.

When I was about eleven years old, Butch (yes, his real name) hit me from behind in a cushion fight. I fell forward and hit my tooth against a steel bed frame. It broke clean off. The dentist made a new tooth and screwed it in its place.

Only thirty years later, while we were in Mozambique, did the tooth start giving me trouble, becoming loose at random times. I was afraid that I was going to lose it, and not caring much for the toothless "pirate look," we had to make a plan. The closest qualified dentist was in a neighboring country, a two days' drive away.

We found the solution. Betsy went to the market and bought some cheap super glue (which, incidentally, contains arsenic!). She promptly glued my tooth back in place. No problem. It lasted for years.

Some time later, while we were in South Africa teaching a cross-cultural course, we took a few Chinese students for a drive. This was just the time that the tooth decided to become loose again. No problem. We stopped at the nearest supermarket, bought a tube of super glue, and stuck it right back in. To the horror of our Chinese friends!

Betsy had to glue that tooth back in place several times over many years. People have asked us why we didn't just go to a dentist when we were in South Africa? Well, we were always so busy, there was never enough time, and to be honest, we just got used to quickly fixing it ourselves.

However, after moving to Southeast Asia, the inevitable happened. One day, while eating my lunch, I took a bite and heard an unpleasant crack in my mouth. The root of my false, glued-in tooth had just cracked. This was a problem not even the glue could fix. I had to find a local dentist. He told me he had to extract the root and put in a new false tooth.

Being from a "participative culture," the dentist called his assistant and his receptionist to observe the event. There I was, in an awkward position on the dentist's chair, slightly distressed, with a numb mouth, and with all these strange and exotic faces hovering above me when he approached me with the pliers.

It sounds a bit like a joke that goes, "How would an Indian dentist, a Chinese assistant, and an Indonesian receptionist pull a tooth?" The answer? "As a team."

He first took out the glue-tooth. That was easy. Then it was time to pull out the root. He almost pulled me right off the seat. The root wasn't budging. The receptionist pushed down on my shoulders to keep me in place. The assistant was extracting the blood and saliva from my mouth. The root didn't budge. Gasps of exertion and exclamations in three languages accompanied the effort, along with my groans in Afrikaans.

Suddenly the stubborn root came out, sending the dentist staggering back, accompanied by a collective and loud exclamation of "waaaaaahhhhh!!" There you have it—cross-cultural dentistry at its finest!

Now we had another problem—trying to figure out how to get the news to the "tooth mouse" (the equivalent of the tooth fairy) in South Africa about this special treasure tooth. We hoped he could send money via PayPal.

"I look like my passport photo!"

Betsy, Southeast Asia

We were visiting our daughter and her family in America and had one more day with them before the grueling 36-hour flight back to Southeast Asia.

"Your flight has been canceled," the upbeat email told me. It almost sounded like a fun announcement—for a split second. I glued myself to the phone, trying to find out what our new itinerary was. Not too bad—we were flying out one day later.

Now I had to dig out some clean underwear from somewhere in the suitcases, which had been packed like a tin of sardines. Where were the days when I could travel with a backpack and a camera? Everything fit in that backpack. A few pieces of clothing, underwear, and toothpaste. That's about it. Now, I could hardly fit in all the medicine, reading glasses, the jersey for cooler weather, and the special walking shoes designed for people with back problems...

The new flight schedule looked good—until we got to the airport. Not good. The new tickets seemed to be for reservations only and were not yet "issued." It took *only* an hour and a half to get the proper tickets. We quickly realized that the new tickets included waiting for a connecting flight for another eleven hours at an airport in a country that didn't allow people from South Africa to transit there—you had to get a transit visa beforehand. Of course, we did not plan it that way—apparently, the airline decided to book us on an adventure, right?

Nevertheless, once we got there we were allowed in. We were stuck in an icy-cold airport, where one banana cost the same as a pair of decent shoes. Cold, hungry and miserable, we were so happy to find a haven—a dedicated area in the airport called "Free Internet." We are reasonably fluent in English, so we thought that it meant we could use the internet there for free. Well, there was *no* internet at all. We realized then that what they meant was that this was an area free of the internet... We *had* to think that, otherwise I would have bought that banana to emotionally eat away my frustration.

I went to the bathroom to, you know, powder my face, when I got the shock of my life. I stumbled out of the bathroom, and with a desperate voice I told Henry, "I look like my passport photo!" How did this happen? I'm one of those people who always look terrible on a passport photo—but it's really not my fault. They make me take off my glasses and tuck my hair behind my ears for the photo. I'm not allowed to smile. Everything is stripped away. It's just me and a camera that doesn't know how to take nice photos. *Bad* camera!

If all else fails, smile

Betsy, Southeast Asia

It sounded like gobbledygook. I had no idea if she was asking me something or telling me something. It could have been something serious like, "There is a tsunami coming," or just

"Where are you from?" I was standing in an Asian market, overwhelmed by the vibrancy of colors and the smells of strange-looking fruit and vegetables. There were people everywhere.

Slaughtered chickens were lying in heaps everywhere. People were expertly chopping off heads, feet and skin. Some advice: Never go to a wet market if you get queasy easily. Henry always says that he won't eat food he has a relationship with—like the chicken we once slaughtered in *ParkingTicket*. They were our chickens, we fed them, so how could we eat them? At least these market chickens were nameless.

I wanted to be nice. "Lord, please give me a word of knowledge," I silently prayed. Nothing came to mind. So I just smiled and walked away. Smile-language 101—smile a lot, use your hands, then smile again.

The "wet market"[26] was overflowing with vegetables and fruit. It was a farmer's market, Asian style. I'd never been to a "dry market" though—I could never find any. It was easy to be mindful of God there—you just had to look at the abundance and variety of produce on display to know that God was the Ultimate Creator. God must have had fun when He made some of those crazy-looking Southeast Asian fruits.

I did not know the names for some of the fruits and vegetables, so I just pointed and smiled again. I think the lady at the vegetable stall asked me if I wanted something. Not sure. Smile, smile some more. I was hopeful that I would graduate to "point and tell" someday.

I very soon realized that some of the people selling produce, had "market English." They could confidently tell

26 An informal market selling fresh foods such as meat, fish, produce and other perishable goods.

you the price of their products, talk a little bit about the mangoes that were in season, and so on. But as soon as I tried to talk about family, or even spiritual stuff, they didn't have the vocabulary.

I was done at the wet market and needed to go to the pharmacy for headache tablets. Again, the gobbledygook. I really needed medicine for headaches. I smiled and pointed at my head. Aha—she smiled back! It seemed I was starting to become fluent in this smile-language. We were making progress. She confidently took me to the shelf with all the hair shampoos. This was interesting. Up to that point, I had never used shampoo to cure a headache. Was this a local remedy? Did I have to drink it or rub it on my forehead? I never tried it though.

I bumped into the aunty who washed the floors at the entrance to our apartment block. I was so frustrated at not being able to communicate with her. I could greet and say two survival phrases. Oh, and I could say that I had two grandchildren. That really helped in emergencies. She loved it when I tried to speak her language. I smiled, she smiled. The thing with this smile-language was that you had to smile with your eyes, not just your mouth. I did a lot of smiling today. She took my hand and said some gobbledygook while smiling broadly. This was a good conversation.

If all else fails, smile...

Training going global

Henry, Southeast Asia

I've written about us teaching the Nations Course in Kenya, where we met those amazing students. Some of them were already in ministry, and others were on their way to start theirs. That specific training course had to be heavily subsidized because the students couldn't afford the fees. We realized that there were so many missionaries who minister in difficult locations without having had any missions training. They may have had theological training, but probably no cross-cultural training. Cross-cultural training includes topics such as how to learn a language as an adult, how to present the gospel in a culturally relevant way, and how to watch for cultural clues that could help spread the gospel faster.

There are many reasons missionaries go without cross-cultural training. The most obvious one is that there is no such training available in their country. Or they simply can't afford to attend in-person training events. Such courses may last from six weeks to a few months, so cost and time are major influencing factors.

Even from our early years in Mozambique, I had a burning in my heart to help missionaries to go to the field well-equipped—to help them be effective in ministry so they could thrive cross-culturally. We saw many new missionaries come to the mission field with a strong calling and full of passion, only to be unable to cope and eventually return to their sending countries, feeling ashamed and defeated. To me this was not only tragic but also avoidable. After observing a number of such missionaries, we realized that they all had one thing in common: a lack of cross-cultural training before entering the mission field.

After moving to Southeast Asia to follow God's clear instruction to go there to train missionaries, I finally started to understand my true calling. All the years of missions experience among the Iso, my experience teaching other missionaries, and even my business and IT experience of years before all came together. Everything fell into place. This was *my* moment of clarity:

THIS IS WHAT I WAS BORN FOR.

Even though I'm not the academic type, I felt an urgency to pursue formal theological education while we were still in Mozambique. I completed a Master of Theology degree part-time while we were living with the Iso. Because we were now trainers, our World Outreach leader Peter Smith challenged me to pursue a doctorate. While working toward my PhD in missiology, God began to download into me the idea of developing online missions training.

Online missions training was unknown at the time. Many of my colleagues were adamant, though—you can't train missionaries online. But when I explained my dream to Bruce, the international director of our missions agency at the time, he listened intently and replied, "This is going to be a game-changer!" This was the final affirmation and encouragement I needed. It was only then that I realized why God had led me into academic studies.

We knew that establishing such a ministry would require all our time and energy. In coordination with Peter, Betsy and I began phasing out of all our leadership positions and roles in World Outreach. Some roles we could hand over immediately, others only after a year, and I committed to my role on the International Leadership for another three years.

And this is how Didasko Missions Academy[27] was born in 2016. It was not just a case of starting to develop courses and posting them online. We had to install and test various Learning Management Systems (LMS), set up separate internet servers for course hosting, develop the public website,

27 Didasko Missions Academy, www.dasko.org

get our email server up and running, and handle many other behind-the-scenes necessities. We formulated our copyright and license agreements, ensuring our courses would remain free for all to access. We wrote our mission and vision statements and designed a privacy policy. We set up a makeshift studio for making videos in a room in our apartment and managed to get the sound and lighting just right. And we developed our first three courses. It was an enormous job, but we launched our first three courses in early 2019.

Again, God's plans and timing are amazing—a few months after we launched Didasko, COVID broke out. Our Southeast Asian country introduced draconian lockdown measures. We learned the COVID language, just like the rest of the world: *SOP* means Standard Operating Procedure, not the Afrikaans word for soup. *Flattening the curve* was not a new diet. *Social distancing* is an oxymoron in my opinion, and apparently there is a difference between *isolation* and *quarantine*.

The old way of doing things was gone. Online training, online meetings, online everything was the new normal. And we were ready with Didasko Missions Academy. Students from all over the world enrolled and completed our courses. By the time COVID ended, Didasko was well-established. This is my God!

"For from Him and through Him and to Him are all things. To Him be the glory forever!" (Romans 11:36).

Durian and chopsticks

Henry, Southeast Asia

In Southeast Asia, I had to overcome a new challenge—eating with chopsticks. I discovered there were muscles in my hands I never knew I had. These muscles tended to go into contraction after multiple failed attempts to get food into my mouth. Whoever came up with the idea of trying to get food into one's mouth by balancing rice grains on two thin chopsticks? Amazingly, it was the same people who built the Great Wall of China, made Ming Dynasty vases, invented gunpowder, and made many more wonderful inventions.

Back to eating utensils. I was relieved to notice that people seemed not to be too offended when I asked for a spoon and fork (no knife and fork there). They seemed, however, to be slightly amused at the foreigner who was struggling to eat with two sticks.

Enough of that. I resolved to learn to eat with chopsticks. I had a practice set in the lounge, so whenever I "lounged" about, I practiced with the sticks. I was sure I would reach a skill level where I could host a YouTube video of myself catching a fly with chopsticks, just like Mr. Miyagi of *The Karate Kid*... NOT!

Eventually, I just gave up and decided that I would just eat with plastic forks and spoons whenever I ate in that uniquely practical Asian invention called the *food court*. No, not the kind you might know in your country—a typical food court in Southeast Asia is essentially a large rectangular area with food stalls all around the outside, surrounding a central area containing plastic tables and chairs where the actual eating is done.

One stall cooks chicken rice, another fish stew, another pig organ soup, and so on. They have lots of choices of all kinds of rice and noodle dishes. I always gave the pig-organ soup a miss. When you went in a group, each person simply went to the stall that cooked the food they wanted, then returned to eat together at a table. Fun!

Then there was durian. Oh yes, *the* durian—the fruit with the most fearsome reputation! It's much beloved by those living in that part of the world—and equally feared by all visitors. There are a few sayings about durian: "Tastes like heaven, smells like hell," and "It smells like a sewer, tastes like custard." Tips for eating included holding your nose while eating… and whatever you do, never burp.

Durian was a mystery to me. Was it already stinky in paradise or did it only become stinky after the Fall? Durian is banned from hotels, banks, public transport, etc. Large "No Durian" signs warn that anyone who dares to bring this fruit inside these buildings will face fines. Why? Well, because the smell tends to linger… and linger…

You could eat this delicacy straight up as a piece of fruit, or you could have durian ice cream, dried durian, durian sweets, durian coffee, durian this, and durian that. Although we ate small pieces of durian and even frozen durian, we never could take the big step of eating a substantial amount like the locals do. That made me think of the missionary saying, "Lord, I'll eat it if You'll keep it down."

Gunmen after midnight

Henry, Southeast Asia

"Wake up! Passports!"

We looked down the barrels of several submachine guns pointing directly at us, held by army and police officers in full gear. I woke up groggy, my heart pounding. My mind was blank. Where are our passports? In fact, where *are* we?

This sounds like something straight out of a movie, right? Nope—just my dear wife and me trying to catch a nap at an airport in Southeast Asia after our flight was delayed. Apparently, there had been some kind of terrorist alert at the airport, and we might have fit the description of the terrorists...

We often had to travel to this part of the world for meetings, even before we eventually moved there. The return flights to South Africa were always scheduled to depart at the brutal hour of 2 a.m. With no public transport available after 10 p.m., unless you were willing to pay exorbitant prices. We had no choice but to arrive at the airport quite early and endure the long wait.

This time, just as we cleared customs and immigration— the point of no return—the announcement came that our flight was delayed until 4 a.m. What were we to do now? With most of the small food stalls closed for the night, we did the only sensible thing we could. We found a row of reasonably comfortable lounge chairs, stretched out, and by some small miracle, fell asleep.

It was around midnight when we were awakened by the police and the army. They swept through the terminal, searching every face and every bag, moving methodically down the rows of weary travelers. After a brief inspection, they decided we weren't the ones they were after and moved on. But there was no going back to sleep after that. It took nearly an hour for our racing hearts to slow and our bodies to stop trembling from the adrenaline.

Many years before, a good friend gave us some wisdom: Before you go on a trip, be "prayed up." Traveling often involves long hours, last-minute crises, delays, and discomfort. Often, the first thing you tend to do is neglect your time with God.

Good advice. If we weren't in a good place with God, that incident would have cost us more than just an accelerated heartbeat.

I have crushed Satan under your feet

Betsy, Southeast Asia

It started off as something quite simple—or so we thought. Just a bladder infection. After a few rounds of medication, the doctor decided I needed an ultrasound. And there it was: a huge lump in my uterus, along with several cysts on my ovaries. Not good news.

I was quickly referred to a specialist. She explained that the uterine tumor absolutely had to be removed—it had no business being there. The ovarian cysts, on the other hand, might burst and clear up on their own, so they weren't as urgent. Surgery was scheduled for the removal of the tumor and everything seemed under control.

Shortly after, I had a dream one night that shook me. It started off as a nightmare. In the dream, Henry and I were walking down a road when a massive snake suddenly appeared from behind the bushes to attack us. I was frozen in fear. I woke up with a shock and in an instant, I was standing beside our bed. My spirit immediately recognized that this was no ordinary dream—it was an attack from the enemy. I began praying, declaring God's protection over me.

As I continued praying, I had a vision. It was as though I was back in my dream, yet I knew I was fully awake. I saw a huge rock falling from heaven, crushing the snake completely. The image was so vivid it was almost funny—the snake's tail wriggled briefly from under the rock before going limp. Then I saw myself climbing on top of the rock. Once I stood on top of it, I realized the rock was no small boulder—it was the size of a mountain. And then I heard the voice of God in my spirit: "I have crushed Satan under your feet."

I knew then that God was assuring me that whatever lay ahead, He was in control.

The surgery went smoothly. The tumor was not cancerous—praise God! Weeks later, the persistent pain in my abdomen revealed that the ovarian cysts were not going to dissolve on their own. They had grown so entwined with my ovaries that the only option was to remove the ovaries entirely. Another surgery.

I had barely returned home after the second surgery when things took a dangerous turn. I developed deep vein thrombosis. The doctor sent me to the emergency room but because it was a national holiday, the medical staff at the ER were very relaxed, in "holiday mode," so they simply gave me blood thinners and sent me home. That night, I woke up with intense pain in my chest and shoulder. Henry rushed back to the hospital. This time, the ER doctor had me admitted. I had suffered a pulmonary embolism. Still, we knew God was in control—He had crushed Satan under my feet, remember.

I eventually returned home—weak, dehydrated, and lethargic. I started walking around the apartment, trying to regain my strength, when I tripped over my own foot and crashed face-first onto the tile floor. And again, God had His people there to help. By another *God-incidence* there was a South African couple living in the same apartment building, just a few floors down, who came to the rescue. This man was a trained paramedic. We were sure he and his wife were angels in disguise. Another trip to the hospital. This time I had a swollen forehead, a broken left elbow, and a badly sprained right hand.

Henry became my full-time caregiver—feeding me, bathing me, and dressing me. He was incredible. Right then, in that place of complete helplessness, I remembered again God's vision and His words to me: "I have crushed Satan under your feet."

No matter how relentless the attacks, no matter how much the enemy tried to steal my health, my peace, and my strength—God had already declared victory. He was in control. Always.

Only later did we realize that the words I'd heard were almost the exact same words from Romans 16:20: "*The God of peace will soon crush Satan under your feet.*" God is good!

The Special Branch for special people

Henry, Southeast Asia

After ten years of living in Southeast Asia, and with Didasko running smoothly, we sensed that God was releasing us to move to America to be closer to our daughter and her family. Since our online ministry only required a reliable internet connection, we were no longer tied to any specific location.

While we were in the long, complicated process of applying for American visas, one requirement loomed over us like a mountain: getting police clearance certificates—proof that we had no criminal record. Straightforward enough you would think, for honest people of course—until we learned that we needed one for every country we had lived in for more than six months. Three countries. Three certificates. Three bureaucratic jungles.

In normal times this would have been daunting. But these weren't normal times. This was COVID. Borders were closed. Offices shuttered. Governments frozen. Everything was in lock-down—everything and everyone, that is, except God.

South Africa was our first hurdle. Normally you need to personally present yourself at a police station in South Africa for fingerprints to be taken, before you can submit your request. But we were living in Southeast Asia at the time. We couldn't fly back to South Africa. That was not possible during the COVID lockdown. By God's grace, we found a company that could acquire the certificates on our behalf. It cost us dearly to courier fingerprints and the required forms to South Africa. Afterwards the coveted certificates had to be couriered back to Southeast Asia. But they arrived. One mountain crossed.

Mozambique looked impossible, too. How could we secure certificates from a government office in a country that we hadn't lived in for over ten years? And even if we got them, they would be in the official language, Portuguese. All of this was during COVID, remember.

Yet God had already gone before us. Lizette, our good friend from our earliest days in Mozambique, stepped in. She lived in Maputo, the capital city of Mozambique. She secured the documents, had them officially translated, notarized, and "by chance," a colleague carried them straight to our city in Southeast Asia during a trip he had planned some time before. At that time limited international flights were available. No coincidences there, only *God-incidences*.

But the most nerve-racking challenge lay right where we were living then—in Southeast Asia itself. Because of COVID, travel outside our neighborhood without police permits was not allowed. To obtain these certificates we would have to acquire local travel permits and travel for six hours to the capital, all the way masked, monitored, and checked at every roadblock.

Confusion awaited us. There were two different types of "good conduct" certificates. We obtained the simpler one, only to be told by the officials there that they suspected America might demand the more advanced version—issued not by them, but by the nation's equivalent of the FBI, the "Special Branch."

So sometime later, we were off again to the capital. Permits. Taxis. Masks. Nervous prayers. When we arrived at the Special Branch headquarters, the reality of it all hit us. This wasn't a process that just required some paperwork. Fingerprints were taken, more documents filled in, and then we were told to wait.

Finally, an officer appeared. He was polite, even kind, but his questions carried weight. That was when it struck us— we were being interrogated. As Christian missionaries in a Muslim nation, the stakes certainly felt much higher. But God gave us the right words, the right answers. Fear gave way to peace, and we managed to remain outwardly calm.

At long last, the officer handed us the precious certificates. We stepped out of that building rejoicing, praising the God who had carried us through every step.

And now for the final twist of irony: In the end, the American consulate required only the easier, simplified certificates—the ones we got first. Oh, well.

But we saw God's hand in every form that we had to fill in, every certificate that we got, and every obstacle we had to overcome. We saw that, although everything was under lockdown, His power was not. His presence never left us—not in visa offices, not in the Special Branch's headquarters, nowhere.

Our God is the same yesterday, today and forever (Hebrews 13:8).

CHAPTER TWELVE

BACK TO THE BEGINNING

⸺◈◈◈⸺

The generator and the witchdoctor

Henry, South Africa

Let's go back to the time when we realized that millions of people still lived without ever hearing the name of Jesus. It was at that time that these words of Jesus became our mission, our goal in life:

> *"Therefore, go and make disciples of all nations, baptizing them in the name of the Father and of the Son and of the Holy Spirit, and teaching them to obey all that I have commanded you. And surely I am with you always, even to the end of the age"* (Matthew 28:19-20).

We were invited to attend a training on the use of the Jesus Film for evangelism. This training was life-changing and prepared us for the future. During the training we learned how to set up the projector, string up a screen, and place loudspeakers so crowds on both sides could watch the life of Jesus told in their own language. We learned how to partner with local pastors so the gospel would take root and spread

235

long after the film was over. Evangelism was no longer just handing out tracts or hoping someone would listen. This was evangelism with impact—showing entire communities the story of Jesus and then inviting them to respond.

The group being trained was a large one. Many of the participants were much taller than I, and I couldn't even get close enough to see the projector being set up. Then the training team brought out a generator—essential for showing the Jesus film in remote areas. The noisy generator would be placed a distance away so the noise wouldn't bother the people watching the film. The trainer warned that thieves sometimes waited in the dark, ready to rip out the cable and run off with the generator. Therefore, every team needed someone willing to guard the generator.

In that moment, a light went on inside me. Here it was at last—my calling! I wasn't tall enough to help with the setup of the projector, I wasn't a fiery evangelist, but I was more than willing to sit on that generator. Nothing would make me budge. Nobody was going to steal it on my watch—because those people needed to see Jesus.

A few weeks after the training, we joined a Jesus Film team. Coen and Denise, an older couple, invited us along on their next outreach, and we were just bursting with excitement. We traveled with them in their pickup truck. On the way, we asked them where the rest of the team was. "You're looking at it," they said. Just the two of them. And now us.

We reached a dusty soccer field and began unloading the equipment. I was ready for generator duty to start fulfilling my God-given calling. But then, much to my dismay, Coen simply parked his truck a small distance away, took out a

236

heavy chain and secured the generator to the truck's bull bar. My calling was gone in the single click of a padlock! I was devastated.

Now visionless, we asked them timidly, "So what can we do to help?" They answered, "Go prayer walking."

We looked at each other—prayer what? We were barely saved and had never been exposed to anything like this. Prayer walking? They explained it simply: Just walk around the perimeter of the field where we were going to show the film and pray. Pray that people would be set free. Pray that many would come to Jesus. Pray for protection. Pray for good weather. This we could do, so that's what we did.

That night, as the Jesus Film played and hundreds watched the story of Jesus, a witchdoctor living at the far end of the field began beating his drum. He was furious. In his spirit he must have known we were encroaching on his spiritual territory. Coen fearlessly walked right up to his house and started praying, warring against evil forces. What an example to us! We were in awe. The witchdoctor didn't like this resistance and set the field on fire. The fire crept closer and closer. People grew restless, their eyes now fixed on the flames edging nearer and not on the movie anymore. Some people got ready to run before the flames surrounded the crowd.

All of a sudden, the fire stopped moving forward. And it stopped exactly where we had walked and prayed. Not an inch further. Our God, the Living God, had drawn a line in the sand that night, and the flames obeyed Him.

When the film ended, many people gave their lives to Christ. There were so many, Coen and Denise told us to start praying for people. Us? We had never done such a thing before. Nervously we prayed for people to be saved, for sick people to be healed, for jobs, and many other requests. Once the ice was broken, we found it was easy to pray for people.

And then, the most astonishing thing happened. The witchdoctor himself came forward, weeping, repenting, surrendering to Jesus. Coen told him to fetch his fetishes, magic charms, and all his witchcraft items that were holding him in bondage and to throw it all into the fire—that same fire he himself had lit. The look of freedom on that man's face was unforgettable.

We had walked onto that soccer field—insecure, inexperienced new believers—but walked off forever changed for having witnessed the power of God.

The stories and testimonies in this book are a dedication to the God who took us on a wild journey with Him, a journey that is still going strong. A journey that started with a generator.

Over the years people have asked us whether we've ever regretted giving up our "old lives"—my beloved profession and the wealth it could potentially have generated or the house and life we left behind. The answer is always a categorical "no, never!" We are living a life of the "long yes."

If God can use a city slicker, computer geek who thought he was only good enough to guard a generator, and a quiet, book-loving librarian who preferred hiding behind shelves, imagine what He can do with *you*. Never despise small beginnings (Zechariah 4:10).

Find *your* "generator."

Say "yes."

Doxology

"Now to Him who is able to keep you from stumbling and to present you unblemished in His glorious presence, with great joy—to the only God our Savior be glory, majesty, dominion, and authority through Jesus Christ our Lord before all time, and now, and for all eternity. Amen" (Jude 1:24-25).

HOW YOU CAN BECOME INVOLVED IN MISSIONS— EVEN FROM YOUR LIVING ROOM

Jesus said, "Go and make disciples of all nations."[28] He meant all of us. He also said, "The harvest is plentiful, but the workers are few."[29] That's still true today. In the next verse He said, "Ask the Lord of the harvest, therefore, to send out workers into His harvest."

Pray for more workers

So here's the first step you can take right now: Pray. Ask the Lord to send out workers to the people groups who still don't know Him. But don't stop there. Prayer opens doors, but action keeps them moving!

Support a "frontier" missionary

These are men and women reaching the "ends of the earth," the Unreached People Groups who have little or no access to the gospel. Most of them don't receive salaries. They rely on

---

28 Matthew 28:19-20
29 Matthew 9:37-38

God's people, like you, to fund them. If you can, commit to giving monthly. They are the most underfunded kind of missionaries, and your partnership can make the difference between them being able to stay in the mission field or having to leave.

Invest in missionary training

Help Didasko equip more missionary candidates through our free, high-quality training. Your contribution to Didasko's Growth Fund enables us to develop new resources, expand our reach, and train more workers for the harvest. Give at www.dasko.org/donate

Go see for yourself

Visit a missionary on the field. You'll never return the same. Prepare for challenges—unfamiliar food, different clothing, even safety concerns. But also prepare for something else— spiritual growth. It's often life changing.

Explore your own calling

If you've ever wondered what it's like to serve cross-culturally, start with our free "Discovering Missions" series at www.dasko.org

Use your skills at home

Not everyone can relocate to other areas or countries, but you can still play a vital role. Missions agencies need accountants, designers, tech specialists, administrators—people with ordinary skills for eternal outcomes. Such work can often be done remotely too.

And there it is in a nutshell: pray, fund, go, and assist. God can use you anywhere!

Henry and Betsy are the founders of Didasko Missions Academy. Didasko's aim is to train Christians to be effective in making Jesus known and glorified among the nations. Their guiding slogan is: "Help develop more effective Kingdom workers." This aims to keep them and their collaborating partners focused on the main task God has given them.

To achieve this goal, they provide missionary training that is "available to anyone, anywhere." They do this by presenting their courses online and by making them available free of charge. The bulk of all their courses is in video format with subtitles in twenty languages.

At time of printing, Christians from over 70 countries have earned course certificates.

www.dasko.org

Consider contributing to Didasko's growth fund by donating at www.dasko.org/donate.

243

Some Didasko student testimonies

"I have never seen a ministry working in love like this: almost all institutions are looking for profit, but Didasko is offering their generosity for us. May God pay back for this excellent job you are doing to feed God's people." (Anonymous student)

"A church-planting team in Thailand, made up mostly of Filipinos, had begun to feel discouraged and lose their sense of direction. During a field visit, my husband and I noticed their struggle and shared several videos from the Strategy module of the Missions101 course. The impact was immediate—fresh vision ignited, passion was rekindled, and the team developed a clear strategy to move forward with renewed confidence." (Ruby, The Philippines)

… "because Didasko's courses use vivid graphics and real-life stories, the concept came alive. We realized this was exactly the kind of breakthrough we need to pursue. From that moment on, the team had clarity, focus, and a strategic path forward." (Missionary team in a restricted country)

"The teachings make me understand my calling better and to do it the best." (Nigerian student)

"After doing the Fruitful Practices course, I was able to develop an outline for applying these fruitful practices in Nigeria, based on the seven themes of fruitfulness."

"The Didasko courses were an answer to prayer." (Ursula, USA)

"I am thankful that Didasko has made these courses free as it enables those who wouldn't be able to afford to do so otherwise engage information that is on par with college and seminary level courses." (Seminary professor, USA)

worldoutreach

World Outreach was established in 1932 by Dr Len Jones. Dr Jones constantly emphasized two priorities: a **tenacious faith in a God who can do great things**, and an expanded vision among people who dare to believe.

One thing that fervently remains the same is the focus to take the gospel to "unreached people" (UPG) groups, who are ethno-linguistic communities who have never heard of Jesus.

Today, there are World Outreach missionaries and co-workers in 70 nations, who seek to reach the unreached peoples across the globe. These passionate missionaries are filled with a vision to fulfill all that God has for their lives and **dare to believe in a God who can do the impossible.**

WE REMAIN

* A faith-based ministry totally dependent on God

* Intercultural

* Pioneering

* Committed to making disciples, and growing and developing leaders

Visit World Outreach's website at https://world-outreach.com

ESTÉ HUPP ART

https://www.estehupp.com/

Esté Hupp is a mixed media painter, illustrator, and creative mentor whose work is rooted in nature, freedom, and faith. Originally from South Africa and now living in Columbus, Ohio, Esté's art is a reflection of her spiritual journey—a blend of beauty, mystery, and connection with nature and the Creator.